Praise for
Ask, Seek, Find

"These excellent, down-to-earth, thought-provoking questions—especially when used in conjunction with actual Book of Mormon study—will lead to much deeper understanding and application of the Book of Mormon in individual lives and open additional opportunities for the Holy Ghost to teach, direct, and inspire. In addition to individual study and family study, these questions will be an invaluable resource for teachers, helping them do a much better job of involving their students in meaningful discussions in their Book of Mormon classes."

—DAVID J. RIDGES
Best-selling author of *The Gospel Study Series*

"Liz Kazandzhy's newest book is one of the best Latter-day Saint books for thought-provoking insights into individual verses of the Book of Mormon. Liz's commentary is expansive and unique, giving us a new way to learn from and better apply the scriptures in our lives. It's different than a doctrinal commentary; rather, it's a formula to broaden your thinking and a tool to help you receive personal revelation. If you are looking for new ways to study and receive personal revelation, I encourage you to read and share this excellent book."

—RICHARD OSTLER
Best-selling author and podcast host,
Listen, Learn & Love

"In *Ask, Seek, Find*, Liz Kazandzhy has assembled the most comprehensive list of scripture-inspired questions I have ever seen. These questions inspire reflection on not just the scriptures themselves but on their relevance to our lives. Furthermore, these questions inspire action as well as deeper thought. I would recommend this study companion to anyone looking to enrich their study of the Book of Mormon."

—SUSAN EASTON BLACK
Retired professor of Church history and doctrine
Brigham Young University

"Sheri Dew has taught, 'If we want to grow spiritually, the Lord expects us to ask questions and seek answers.' *Ask, Seek, Find* helps individuals and families do just that as they study the Book of Mormon. Author Liz Kazandzhy has compiled thought-provoking questions that can be used to prompt gospel conversations in the family or to provide individuals food for thought and pondering. It is simple to read and enables readers to look for specific questions by book and chapter! I highly recommend *Ask, Seek, Find* for added *Come, Follow Me* support in 2024."

—REBECCA IRVINE
Author of *Let's Learn Together: New Testament*

"As a reader who loves to feast on the scriptures, I encountered Liz Kazandzhy's book *Ask, Seek, Find* as a refreshing new way to study the scriptures. Kazandzhy has a gift of bringing thought-provoking and open-ended questions to a person's scripture study. There are plenty of commentaries on the shelves that hold another's opinions and insights, but few allow readers to truly seek and find for themselves.

This paragraph from her introduction spoke to me as she reminisced about her time in seminary:

> Above all, I remember the *questions*—questions that prompted answers, and answers that gave way to revelation. Each response that I scrawled into my notebook felt like a layer of conviction being poured onto my spiritual foundation. By the glowing light of my desk lamp, I'd often study late into the night, losing myself in the things of eternity and finding myself in the process.

I truly believe that you too can find 'the things of eternity' as you utilize this workbook."

—RAMONA SIDDOWAY
Author of *We are Adam*

"If you're looking for a way to take your scripture study from *meh* to *WOW!*, this book is the answer. Each question prompts you to apply gospel principles to your life in a way that strengthens the spiritual light inside of you. After all, scripture study is less about information and more about conversion, and these inspired questions help do just that. I've started using these questions while reading the Book of Mormon with my kids, and it has made our discussions so much richer and more spiritually rewarding. Don't wait to up your scripture study game—get this book!"

—SUSIE MCGANN
Author of *You on Purpose*

· BOOK OF MORMON ·

ASK, SEEK, FIND

1,000 QUESTIONS TO DEEPEN YOUR SCRIPTURE STUDY

· BOOK OF MORMON ·

ASK, SEEK,

FIND

1,000 QUESTIONS TO DEEPEN YOUR SCRIPTURE STUDY

LIZ KAZANDZHY

CFI
An imprint of Cedar Fort, Inc.
Springville, Utah

ISBN 13 Paperback: 978-1-4621-4471-6
ISBN 13 Ebook: 978-1-4621-4472-3

Published by CFI, an imprint of Cedar Fort, Inc.
2373 W. 700 S., Suite 100, Springville, UT 84663
Distributed by Cedar Fort, Inc., www.cedarfort.com

Library of Congress Registration Number: 2023941143

Cover design by Shawnda Craig
Cover design © 2023 Cedar Fort, Inc.
Edited by Krissy Barton
Typeset by Liz Kazandzhy

Printed in the United States of America

10 9 8 7 6 5 4 3 2 1

Printed on acid-free paper

To my early-morning seminary teachers.
Thank you for never giving up on me.

CONTENTS

INTRODUCTION

I HAVE NEVER BEEN A MORNING PERSON. AS A kid, I'd stay up late reading or daydreaming, and as a teenager, my first-period classes racked up far more absences than any others. I still managed to keep up with my schoolwork, but there was one thing I could *not* keep up with: early-morning seminary.

Try as I might, my seminary attendance was sporadic at best and, at worst, nonexistent for weeks at a time. "The spirit indeed [was] willing, but the flesh [was] weak" (Matthew 26:41), especially when it came to trading in my warm, cozy bed for a cold seat in a frosty car at the crack of dawn.

It wasn't long before my freshman seminary teacher introduced me to the idea of seminary make-up work, giving me a chance to redeem myself for my many absences. By following along with an at-home seminary manual and answering the questions posed in that manual, I could raise my statistics high enough for seminary graduation. For whatever reason, I was determined to graduate, so this proved to be the perfect solution. Thus began a four-year endeavor of doing make-up work off and on as my early-morning attendance waxed and waned.

The first time I opened my seminary manual, I wasn't sure what to expect. Would the work be so intense that waking up at 5:30 a.m. would seem like a breeze in comparison? Would it be so boring that I'd fall asleep instead of studying,

perhaps actually helping me to wake on time for seminary the next morning? To my surprise, it was neither of those things. The work was doable and enlightening. I remember the helpful illustrations and graphics, the clear definitions of obscure words and phrases, and the powerful quotes from Church leaders confirming the scriptural messages.

But above all, I remember the *questions*—questions that prompted answers, and answers that gave way to revelation. Each response that I scrawled into my notebook felt like a layer of conviction being poured onto my spiritual foundation. By the glowing light of my desk lamp, I'd often study late into the night, losing myself in the things of eternity and finding myself in the process.

Years later—after I had indeed graduated from seminary, by the way—I found myself in another situation that required early-morning attendance: parenthood. It was April of 2015, and my new, adorable alarm clock was named Katya Kazandzhy. And unfortunately, there's no sleeping through the cries of a hungry newborn.

While motherhood left me with a lack of sleep, it provided me with an abundance of time. (At least in the infant phase—not so much later on!) I had recently graduated from college, and I had quit my job when Katya was born, so I now had more free time than I knew what to do with. Eventually, I decided that I wanted to really delve into the gospel, much like I did back in my seminary days. And remembering how much I loved the questions in the seminary manuals, I searched the internet to find something similar:

- "question guide for the Book of Mormon"
- "verse-by-verse question commentary for the scriptures"
- "scripture study questions for the Book of Mormon"

Surely there had to be something, right? But to my amazement, there wasn't.

If I did find questions related to the Book of Mormon, they were usually factual and presented with the answers alongside them. I didn't want factual questions with one right answer—I wanted open-ended questions with answers that I'd have to search my own soul for. I found plenty of verse-by-verse commentaries offering doctrinal explanations and historical insights, but I didn't want that—I wanted questions that would spark my own insights and make me ponder my own spiritual history. After searching long and hard and still coming up empty, the Spirit eventually whispered to me, "Why don't *you* write it?"

And that was the question that started it all.

Over the next few years, I combed through the Book of Mormon, coming up with thought-provoking questions for nearly every verse, leading to a grand total of more than 10,000 questions—1,000 of which are included in this book. I didn't know that my goal to "really delve into the gospel" would end up being so time-intensive, but it was worth it. And not just for my sake but for yours—because now *you*, dear reader, have what *I* wish I had years ago.

Now, before you begin your question-answering journey, I want to give you a few tips about how best to use this book and how it can most benefit you.

As an Individual

First, this book can help you deepen your personal scripture study. The ideal way to use these questions is to write down your answers whenever you have the chance. As Elder Richard G. Scott counseled, "Write down in a secure place the important things you learn from the Spirit. You will find that as you write down precious impressions, often more will come. Also, the knowledge you gain will be available throughout your life."[1] Keep in mind that you can record your thoughts in whatever format is most convenient for you, whether that be in a physical journal, in a document on your computer, or by using a note-taking app on your phone.

Unfortunately, in the busyness of our day-to-day lives, it can be hard to find the time to do this. If that's the case for you, don't beat yourself up. There's still a lot of power in simply pondering your answers and letting "the solemnities of eternity rest upon your [mind]" (Doctrine and Covenants 43:34).

Here are some ways you can implement this book in your personal study:

- After reading the scriptures, choose a set of questions from a chapter you studied, and then ponder and record your answers.
- Pick a question in the morning and think about your answer throughout the day.
- Keep this book in your car and choose a question to ponder during your commute or while running errands.
- Consider writing your own book of "1,000 Answers," either for yourself or for your posterity.

As a Family or Other Group

Second, this book can encourage you to have more meaningful gospel discussions with others.

Just as the *Come, Follow Me* manual encourages group study—whether it be with a spouse, children, roommates, neighbors, or others—this book can also be a valuable tool to prompt enlightening gospel discussions with others.

Consider the following possibilities:

- After studying a chapter together, choose a set of questions to discuss from that chapter.
- Pick a question to discuss at the dinner table, before bed, or on a long drive.
- Have a family member select a question beforehand, think about it, and share their thoughts during a home evening lesson.
- Pose a question on social media, share your answer, and encourage others to share theirs.

IN A CLASSROOM SETTING

Finally, if you have a teaching calling, this book can help you make your lessons more impactful. A teacher who asks quality questions during a lesson is usually far more effective than one who lectures the whole time. As the popular phrase goes, "It's better to be a guide on the side than a sage on the stage." Encouraging students to ponder and answer questions will help guide them to find personal meaning in the gospel.

Here are some tips for using questions in a classroom setting:

- Avoid asking questions that have obvious answers, factual answers, or a specific answer you're looking for. (Thankfully, all the questions in this book avoid these common pitfalls.)
- Learn to be comfortable with silence after posing a question. Allow enough time for students to ponder and possibly gather the courage to answer.

- Don't ask students to answer personal questions out loud. For example, if a question asks, "What sins are you struggling with right now?" a better alternative would be "What are some sins people struggle with in our day?" On the other hand, asking general questions (or questions that ask about past spiritual experiences) is usually okay.
- Do ask students to answer personal questions in their minds or by taking notes on their phone or on a piece of paper. For example, during the last five minutes of your lesson, you could put on some calm Church music, pose a personal question (like 3 Nephi 25:3 in this book), and ask them to record their thoughts.

FINAL THOUGHTS

In any of these contexts, please also take advantage of the Topical Guide in the back of this book, which organizes the questions into over 200 topics. Whether you want to study a certain subject on your own, or you're giving a lesson on a specific topic at home or at church, the Topical Guide can be a wonderful resource to help you in your goals.

Also, as a word of caution, it can be tempting to read and answer these questions without ever looking up the verses they refer to. However, try to resist this urge. Yes, there's power in the questions, but nothing can match the power that comes from the pure word of God contained in the Book of Mormon. So, every time you want to answer a question, make it a goal to also read the accompanying verse and familiarize yourself with its context.

Finally, I wish you the very best as you use these 1,000 questions to delve into the gospel of Jesus Christ. May you lose yourself in the things of eternity and find yourself in the process!

"To ask and to answer questions is at the heart of all learning and teaching."

—President Henry B. Eyring[2]

THE FIRST BOOK OF NEPHI

1 NEPHI 1

V.5: Who do you think needs your prayers right now, whether they are those who are struggling with sin and those who are struggling with trials? What can you do to help them?

V.16: Lehi received revelation in the form of visions and dreams. In what ways have you received revelation throughout your life, and how do you receive it most often? Why do you think different people receive revelation in different ways?

1 NEPHI 2

V.1–2: Have you ever had an experience in which the Spirit warned you of danger and protected you? What do such promptings usually feel like to you?

V.19: What do you think "lowliness of heart" means? What would that look like in your own life right now?

1 NEPHI 3

V.5: How can parents help their children know what commands come from them and which come from the Lord? Why is it important that children know that commandments are from the Lord and not just from their parents?

V.22–23: Considering how much Nephi was willing to pay to have access to the scriptures, how much *time* are you "paying" each day to study them? How could you improve your scripture study?

V.31: When have you faced obstacles in your life that seemed insurmountable? How does faith in Jesus Christ help you to overcome such obstacles?

1 NEPHI 4

V.1: Consider the trials you're going through in your life right now. Then fill in the blank of this sentence with the trial you're facing: "For behold [the Lord] is mightier than all the earth, then why not mightier than _____?" How will keeping the commandments allow the Lord to help you?

V.17: Nephi recognized this moment as an answer to his prayer. When was the last time you remember having a prayer answered, and how did God answer it?

1 Nephi 5

V.2–3: How does stress affect our thoughts, words, and actions, especially in family life? What helps you manage stressful situations and become calm again? How can you be more understanding and helpful when others are stressed?

V.21–22: How have the scriptures been of worth to you as you've journeyed throughout your life? How has your attitude about them changed?

1 Nephi 6

V.4: What are some of your favorite stories and verses from the Book of Mormon? How do those persuade people, and particularly you, to come unto God?

1 Nephi 7

V.1–3: Before traveling to the promised land, the sons of Nephi needed to be married. Likewise, before obtaining exaltation, we must also be married. How do marriage and family prepare us for exaltation? Why is a temple marriage a requirement for exaltation?

V.14: The people of Jerusalem lost the Spirit because they rejected the prophets. What causes people to lose the Spirit in today's world? In your own life, what things cause you to lose the Spirit the most often, and what can you do to avoid those things?

1 Nephi 8

V.10: Lehi was able to see from afar off that the fruit of the tree "was desirable to make one happy." What do you think nonmembers see in our examples that show that the gospel is desirable? What example do you think you're setting for others about how the gospel affects your life?

V.20: In what ways is the gospel path narrow? How do people try to "broaden" that path today, denying the narrowness of it?

V.34: An important part of not heeding the voice of the world is to heed the voice of God. What helps you to care more about what God thinks than what others think?

1 Nephi 9

V.3–4: In a few sentences or paragraphs, how would you describe the history of your life temporally? Also, in a few sentences or paragraphs, how would you describe the history of your life spiritually? Which do you consider more beneficial for your posterity and why? What is the value of each of these versions of your life?

1 Nephi 10

V.6: How have you noticed your own lost and fallen state? How have you relied on the Redeemer, and how have you seen His power redeem and change you?

V.19: What do you think "diligently seeking" entails? What resources are we blessed with in our seeking? What mysteries of God, either related to the scriptures or to your own life, would you most like to have revealed to you?

1 Nephi 11

V.8–9: In addition to his father's description of the fruit as white and desirable, Nephi uses the words *beauty* and *precious* to describe the fruit of the tree. Why is the gospel, and especially the love of God, beautiful to you? Why is it precious? What other words would you use to describe the love of God?

V.28: What are your favorite parables or teachings that Christ taught during His ministry, and why?

1 Nephi 12

V.10–11: Consider the symbolic imagery that "their garments are made white in his blood" and "these are made white in the blood of the Lamb." Though at first this seems illogical, why is it an appropriate symbol for the Atonement of Jesus Christ?

V.18: What causes people to be prideful today, and what "vain imaginations" do they have? What are your personal triggers for pride, and how are you trying to overcome them?

1 Nephi 13

V.4: Elder Bruce R. McConkie taught, "The titles *church of the devil* and *great and abominable church* are used to identify all . . . organizations of whatever name or nature—whether political, philosophical, educational, economic, social, fraternal, civic, or religious—which are designed to take men on a course that leads away from God and his laws and thus from salvation in the kingdom of God."[3] What organizations can you think of that fit this description? How do they lead away from God and His laws?

V.37: How are you seeking to bring forth Zion in your family, your callings, and in other areas of your life? What talents has the Lord given you specifically which you can use to help build Zion during your lifetime?

1 Nephi 14

V.4: Once somebody becomes captive to the devil by giving in to temptations, what tools does Satan use to *keep* them captive? What helps you get out of your "spiritual lows" when you aren't doing what you should spiritually?

V.10: Stephen E. Robinson, a BYU Professor, taught, "Individual orientation to the Church of the Lamb or to the great and abominable church is not by membership but by loyalty. Just as there are Latter-day Saints who belong to the great and abominable church because of their loyalty to Satan and his life-style, so there are members of other churches who belong to the Lamb because of their loyalty to him and his life-style. Membership is based more on who has your heart than on who has your records."[4] How would you describe a member of The Church of Jesus Christ of Latter-day Saints who is part of the church of the devil? How would you describe a nonmember who is part of the Church of the Lamb of God?

1 Nephi 15

V.9: How would you respond to someone who believes that they're too insignificant for God to answer their prayers and give them revelation?

V.35–36: What do people gain temporally from wickedness in this life? What do they lose in the eternities?

1 NEPHI 16

V.2: How do you react when you hear something that "[cuts you] to the very center," like when somebody points out a sin or weakness of yours or tells you that you're wrong? What's the best way to react in a situation like this? How does the Lord want you to react, and how does Satan want you to react?

V.23: Instead of simply complaining like the rest of his family, Nephi took initiative and made another bow and arrow to hunt with. If you are in difficult circumstances right now, what can you do personally to improve your situation? How can the Lord help you in your endeavors?

V.36: The fact that some members of Lehi's family often had the thought of returning to Jerusalem can be compared with the notion that some people often have the thought of returning to previous wicked ways, even while currently keeping the commandments. Why is it so important to completely forsake our sins when we repent of them, and what helps you to do so? How can we change our desires so that "we have no more disposition to do evil, but to do good continually" (Mosiah 5:2)?

1 NEPHI 17

V.7: Often in the scriptures, mountains are symbols for the temple. Why is the temple such a wonderful place to receive direction from the Lord? When are you going to the temple next, and what kind of direction or revelation could you seek there?

V.20: Compare Laman and Lemuel's interpretation of their journey in the wilderness with Nephi's response found in verses 1–3 of this chapter. Why did these two views differ so much? What is the difference between optimists and pessimists, and how does the gospel of Jesus Christ help us to be optimists?

V.39: Why is it important to always remember that God is higher than us? What does He see and know that we don't?

V.47: How do you cope with the anguish that comes from seeing the sins of the world, and especially, seeing the sins of your loved ones?

1 NEPHI 18

V.1: What direction has the Lord given you "from time to time" regarding your family life, educational or career goals, and other important aspects of your life? What is an example in your life when the Lord has guided you one step at a time? Why do you think He does this instead of giving us all the answers at once?

V.12: How does contention in the home halt the progress of the family and individual family members? What can you do to avoid contention in your home? If it does happen, what can you do to resolve it quickly?

1 NEPHI 19

V.6: How do you deal with your own weaknesses that cause you to err? How can you accept your mortal, imperfect self while still striving to be better?

V.23: What are some strategies that you've heard of or used personally that help you to "liken the scriptures unto [yourself], that it might be for [your] profit and learning"?

1 NEPHI 20

V.10: What are some of the most difficult trials you have experienced in your life? How have each of these trials refined your character? What Christlike attributes did you acquire or develop as a result of those trying times?

V.20: What helps you to "live in the world, but not of the world"? What can you do in your own home to make it a refuge from the wickedness of the outside world (here represented as Babylon and the Chaldeans)?

1 NEPHI 21

V.2: Joseph Smith made the statement, "I am like a huge, rough stone rolling down from a high mountain; and the only polishing I get is when some corner gets rubbed off by coming in contact with something else . . . all hell knocking off a corner here and a corner there. Thus I will become a smooth and polished shaft in the quiver of the Almighty."[5] With this example of "polishing" in mind, what experiences have you had in your own life that have polished you and helped you be a better instrument in the hands of the Lord?

V.5: All of the prophets, and especially Jesus Christ, were foreordained for their missions on Earth. What do you think you were foreordained to do? What do you think your life mission entails, and how could you find out?

V.22: How does the Church act as a standard to the world today? When have your standards differed from those of the world, and what has helped you most to keep your standards high throughout your life, especially in the face of peer pressure?

1 NEPHI 22

V.13–14: Though Israel will ultimately prevail, the period described in these verses can seem very dark and gloomy. What helps you to handle the often dark and gloomy state of the world today? What are some things that can lift your spirits when you are feeling troubled about what's happening in the world now?

V.30: How has your study of the scriptures helped you be obedient throughout your life? What have you been reading lately, and how can you apply it to become more obedient to the commandments of God?

"I am convinced that each of us, at some time in our lives, must discover the scriptures for ourselves—and not just discover them once, but rediscover them again and again."

—President Spencer W. Kimball[6]

THE SECOND BOOK OF NEPHI

2 NEPHI 1

V.13: How would you describe the "deep . . . sleep of hell" that Lehi mentions here, and how is it manifested in our day? Why are "awful chains" an accurate representation of wickedness? How do you shake these off when you find yourself bound by them?

V.20: What does this verse look like in your own life? What is your life like when you keep the commandments, and what is it like when you don't keep the commandments?

2 NEPHI 2

V.3: What service do you want to give God during your lifetime?

V.18: This verse represents a half-truth by Satan; the phrase "ye shall not die" was a lie, but "ye shall be as God, knowing good and evil" was true. Why does Satan often use this tactic instead of lying completely? What are some other examples of half-truths he tells people to try to get them to sin?

2 NEPHI 3

V.13: How would you respond to someone who was in shock that God would restore the gospel through a simple boy? What weaknesses have you seen be made strong in your life with the help of the Lord?

V.20: Why is it important to preach the gospel of Christ, even when you don't see immediate results and might never see results? What experiences do you have with this?

2 NEPHI 4

V.24: What does it mean to you to "wax bold in mighty prayer"? What do sincere prayers sound like? What do insincere prayers sound like?

V.31: What trials and weaknesses would you like to overcome in your life right now? How could you enlist the Lord's help to do this?

2 NEPHI 5

V.19: What qualities do you think are most important in a leader or a teacher? What leaders and teachers have you looked up to in your life, and why?

V.26: In what callings have you served in the Church? Which has been the most difficult? Which have been the most rewarding? How have you felt the Lord's support as you've sought to fulfill your callings?

2 Nephi 6

V.3: Why should this (being "desirous for the welfare of your souls") be the motivating factor in teaching and serving? What are some less honorable reasons people teach or serve? What helps us stay focused on the welfare of souls?

V.11: How does God watch over His children who stray? What can we do to watch over them and help them return to the fold? Why should we never give up hope in them?

2 Nephi 7

V.1: How does sin lead us to separate ourselves from God?

V.2–3: What are some of the most miraculous things that the Lord has done or could do? With those miracles in mind, what can He do for you regarding your sins, weaknesses, and trials if you trust in Him?

2 Nephi 8

V.7–8: What are some examples of reproach and reviling that Saints in the latter days must deal with? Why shouldn't we fear them?

V.25: The invitation to arise and then sit down bears the symbol of arising from the dust and being seated on a throne as royalty. What does the gospel teach us about our identity, our worth, and our destiny? What does it mean to you to live up to that?

2 Nephi 9

V.27: What are some ways people waste the days of their probation (i.e., their mortal life)? What are the biggest time-wasters in your life, and what can you do to be more focused on God and more fully keep His commandments?

V.42: Ultimately, those who look down on others will be looked down upon by God. What helps you to avoid looking down on others, especially when you have more money, education, or opportunities than them?

2 Nephi 10

V.14: How can we make God our king? What other things or people do we allow to rule our lives sometimes?

V.15: How does trying to hide our sins affect our relationship with God and others?

V.23: Consider your actions of the last few days. What choices have led you closer to eternal life? If you have made choices that have led you closer to eternal death, what do you need to do to repent of and forsake those things?

2 Nephi 11

V.7: What do you think it would have been like to live during the time of the Savior? How would it be similar to living the gospel now, and how would it be different?

2 Nephi 12

V.18: What can you do to destroy the idols (things that take your focus, time, and money away from God) in your own life?

2 Nephi 13

V.1: This verse can be interpreted as the spiritual drought that covered the world during the Great Apostasy. What important doctrines (bread and water) were misunderstood or unavailable during this time? How do these restored truths provide the world spiritual nourishment in our day?

V.14–15: In what ways do people "grind the faces of the poor"? How do you treat the poor and the needy, and what more might you do to help them?

2 Nephi 14

V.4: The phrases "washed away" and "purged" suggest the intense process of repentance. How else would you describe repentance—both the difficult process and the sweet reward? How often do you repent, and what is that process like for you?

2 Nephi 15

V.5: To destroy the vineyard, the Lord only needed to withhold His protective power from it. How does sinning "turn off" the power of God in our lives? How does repentance turn it back on?

V.12: When does entertainment change from being a good or neutral thing to being something that is considered a sin? How can these things distract us from the work of the Lord?

2 Nephi 16

V.7: How do you feel when "thine iniquity is taken away" after sincere repentance? How can you improve the quality and frequency of your repentance process?

2 Nephi 17

V.1–2: This chapter talks about three countries led by three kings—Syria led by Rezin, Israel led by Pekah, and Judah led by Ahaz. Ahaz had heard that Syria and Israel had become allies in an attempt to seize Jerusalem (Judah's capital), and he and his people began to be very afraid. When in your life have you experienced fear, especially regarding what would happen in the future? How does fear negatively influence our lives?

V.8–9: Syria and Israel were led by mortal men and would ultimately fail. Judah, on the other hand, had the opportunity to be led with the Lord at its head. But this was dependent on their faith, for "if you will not believe, surely ye shall not be established" (v.9). What does it mean to you to live a life that is led by the Lord? What can you do to make Him the "head" (leader) of your life? What other things might people be led by, and why will these things ultimately fail?

2 Nephi 18

V.9–10: In modern language, these verses can be interpreted as something similar to, "Go ahead, try to defeat us! No matter what you do, you won't win because God is with us." How much faith and hope do you have that you can succeed in life with God's help? What enemies (weaknesses, trials, etc.) are you facing, or might you face in the future, that can be defeated with God's help? What are you doing every day to enlist the help of God in your life?

V.11–13: These verses summarize the main theme of these historical chapters of Isaiah: do not trust in or fear man; trust in and fear the Lord. What does it mean to you to trust in man versus in the Lord? What does it mean to you to fear man versus the Lord?

2 Nephi 19

V.6: What is your favorite title of Jesus Christ found in this verse, and why? How have these descriptions manifested themselves in your life and in your relationship with the Savior?

V.18: How is wickedness like a burning fire? How can wickedness spread from one person to another? On the other hand, how can righteousness spread from one person to another?

2 Nephi 20

V.7–12: Because of Assyria's military and political success, the nation would be lifted up in pride and take glory upon itself and its idols. When you have success in your life, what helps you remain humble? What are the dangers of being lifted up in pride and considering our success our own instead of the Lord's?

V.26: Wickedness will eventually be overcome. How does the Atonement of Jesus Christ help us overcome personal wickedness? What advice would you give somebody who is trying to overcome a sin in their life?

2 Nephi 21

V.13: How does envy affect relationships? How does contention affect relationships? What can you do to decrease the contention and envy in your own life?

2 Nephi 22

V.3: What are some properties and purposes of water? How is this like the Savior's role in our lives?

2 Nephi 23

V.15: What do you think the phrase "joined to the wicked" entails? What can we do to separate ourselves from the wicked, and wickedness, in the world today?

2 Nephi 24

V.2: Who are some examples in your life of Church members who have come from "the ends of the earth"? How does it make you feel to know that the Church of Jesus Christ is truly a worldwide church?

V.11: What are some things that people strive for in this life that they cannot take with them into the eternities? What can we take with us, and what are you doing to treasure those things?

2 NEPHI 25

V.9: How does iniquity get passed down from one generation to another? What are some examples you've seen of this? What does it take for a person to break this cycle of iniquity and destruction?

V.26: What do you do to "talk of Christ" in your own life? What are some reasons you "rejoice in Christ"? When was the last time you preached of Christ—what did you teach to whom? Who might need to hear you "preach of Christ" next?

2 NEPHI 26

V.8: What persecutions have you faced throughout your life as a result of your faith? What has helped you keep the faith despite these difficulties? How has hearkening unto the words of the prophets and centering your life on Christ brought blessings to your life?

V.26: What can you do to help people feel more welcomed at church? What attitude should you have toward others who attend church, even those who seem unconventional or like they don't adhere to the Church's standards? Why doesn't the Lord deny people entrance to His houses of worship (and why should we follow His example)?

2 NEPHI 27

V.11: How does someone read the scriptures "by the power of Christ"? What scripture study methods have worked for you to make your study spiritual and effective? What are some ways that you receive revelation from your scripture study?

V.14: What are some reasons that people reject the Book of Mormon? What responses do you have for each of these arguments?

2 NEPHI 28

V.7–8: Another false belief in the last days is that we need not worry about the consequences of sin, especially "a little sin." Why is this such a dangerous teaching? What is wrong with the concept of God presented in verse 8? Why is there no such thing as "a little sin," and what could happen if we start rationalizing our sins?

V.29: Contrary to this verse, what could you do to seek out more of the word of God? What scriptures are you less familiar with that you could make it a point to study? What doctrines would you like to learn more about? How well do you utilize other Church resources, like the Church magazines and lesson manuals?

2 NEPHI 29

V.3: When have you heard this from other people? What are some explanations you can give about why we have the Book of Mormon and not just the Bible? What testimony could you share about how having the Book of Mormon, and not just the Bible, has blessed your life?

2 Nephi 30

V.7: How does the gospel make you more of a "delightsome" person? How have you seen the positive effects of the gospel in the lives of others?

V.16–17: Nobody can keep anything from the Lord, and in the last days, all that was in the dark will be brought to light. How do you think people will feel when their evil works are discovered? Is there anything in your life that you're trying to keep secret or in the dark? If so, why? What could you do to come clean, both with the Lord and with others as needed?

2 Nephi 31

V.11: How would you explain the concept of repentance, and why we need it, to a child? How would you explain baptism in the same way?

V.13: How is the Holy Ghost like a fire? What role does He play in the development of our testimonies, and how does He help us live according to that which we know?

2 Nephi 32

V.9: What are some ways that we can fulfill the command to "pray always"? What are some endeavors or activities that are important to you right now? How could you incorporate prayer in those aspects of your life so that the Lord "will consecrate thy performance unto thee, that thy performance may be for the welfare of thy soul"?

2 Nephi 33

V.15: As Nephi's record began, so it ended—with a declaration of unwavering obedience. Reflecting on Nephi's life and writing, what characteristics did he have that stand out to you? What are your favorite parts of First and Second Nephi, and why? What could you do to follow Nephi's righteous example?

"No message appears in scripture more times, in more ways than 'Ask, and ye shall receive.'"

—President Boyd K. Packer[7]

THE BOOK OF JACOB

JACOB 1

V.17: What errands have you obtained from the Lord? These could be church callings, educational and career endeavors encouraged by the Spirit, creating and raising an eternal family, God-inspired use of your talents, etc. How are you doing at fulfilling them?

JACOB 2

V.5: What role do our thoughts play in how we behave? Why do you think we'll be judged for our thoughts and not just our actions (see Alma 12:14)? What good thoughts can you use to replace your bad thoughts when they happen to come into your mind?

V.18–19: Thinking about your primary reasons for wanting to make money, how consistent are these reasons with building the kingdom of God and serving others? What are some things you'd like to do with your money or talents that will help build God's kingdom?

V.34: What commandments are you fully aware of but fail to keep consistently? Why do you disobey them, and what do you need to do or change in order to obey them?

JACOB 3

V.1: What afflictions has the Lord consoled you in throughout your life?

V.11: When you start to experience spiritual apathy (i.e., take on a casual attitude toward the gospel and commandments), what can you do to "arouse the faculties of your soul," "shake yourselves," and "awake" from that spiritual slumber? What helps you stay spiritually engaged and alert?

JACOB 4

V.7: How is our relationship with God strengthened because of our weakness as mortals? What have your own weaknesses taught you about God's grace?

V.13: When has the Spirit spoken to you about "things as they really are, and of things as they really will be"? Is there anything you're worried about right now that might be relieved by praying for knowledge from the Holy Ghost?

JACOB 5

V.20: The Lord spent considerable time nourishing the various branches of Israel (His "other sheep"), such as the Nephites, and they brought forth considerable fruit. Up to this point in your life, how has the Lord nourished you, both physically and spiritually? What fruits have you brought forth to Him in return?

V.65–66: Applying these verses to us individually instead of to the house of Israel as a whole, why is it important to gradually try to overcome our sins and weaknesses rather than trying to do it "all at once"? During your lifetime, how have you seen the good in yourself grow while the bad has been cleared away?

V.75: This verse teaches that diligence, obedience, and service lead to joy with the Savior. In what specific ways have you seen this in your own life?

JACOB 6

V.4: Elder Quentin L. Cook used the terms "roots and branches" to highlight the importance of family history work, with roots referring to our ancestors and branches referring to our descendants.[8] How involved are you in family history work (remembering your roots), and what concrete steps can you take to become more actively and consistently involved? How involved are you in seeking to create and maintain an eternal family (remembering your branches), and how can you be better at this?

V.8: In what ways is the plan of redemption being mocked today?

V.12: How is being wise different than being smart?

JACOB 7

V.18: Sherem admits that he was deceived by Satan; however, he ultimately made the choice to be deceived. As Elder Larry L. Lawrence taught, "Jesus votes for us, Satan votes against us, and we cast the deciding vote."[9] How can we avoid being deceived by the power of the devil?

V.24: What means are there "to reclaim and restore" the less active, and what can you do to participate more fully in those reactivation efforts? Is there anyone who is less active who you are close to and on whom you might have an impact?

THE BOOKS OF ENOS, JAROM, AND OMNI

ENOS 1

V.3: Enos received this revelation while alone in nature. Does nature play a role in your spiritual life, and if so, how? Do you have a secluded place where you can go to meditate and receive revelation?

V.5–6: When sins are forgiven, it is guilt that is swept away, not necessarily the memory of the sins or even their consequences. When have you felt your guilt swept away? Are you harboring any guilt that could be lifted by Christ's Atonement through sincere repentance, and if so, how would you feel to have that swept away?

V.26: What about the gospel makes you rejoice? How much have you shared those thoughts and your joy with your family members, ward members, friends, neighbors, and others?

JAROM 1

V.5: How are you doing in your Sabbath day observance? What about your choice of language? If needed, what changes can you make to obey these commandments more fully?

OMNI 1

V.17: Because the Mulekites did not bring scriptures, they lost their testimonies and knowledge of their Creator. Likewise, those who stop studying the scriptures are also in danger of losing their testimonies. Why do you think this is? What is the quality and quantity of your scripture study like, and is there anything you can do to improve it?

THE WORDS OF MORMON

WORDS OF MORMON 1

V.14: Several times in the Book of Mormon it is noted when people go forth "in the strength of the Lord." What does that phrase mean to you? What does that look like in your own life?

"When we read the scriptures with a question in mind and with a sincere desire to understand what Heavenly Father wants us to know, we invite the Holy Ghost to inspire us."

—Come, Follow Me[10]

THE BOOK OF MOSIAH

MOSIAH 1

V.1: What do you do to promote and maintain peace in your home?

V.8: What are some of the most important things you want to teach your children in this life?

V.14: What would this verse look like applied to your own life? "If [the Lord] had not extended his arm" in my life by _____, then I would have _____.

MOSIAH 2

V.3: Prior to receiving the words of their prophet, the people offered sacrifices. What could you sacrifice (sins, bad habits, etc.) in order to be more receptive and worthy of the Holy Ghost in your life, especially during your church meetings?

V.11: What can we do to support our Church leaders in spite of their weaknesses and imperfections? Why is it important to avoid fault-finding in our leaders?

V.36: What choices do you make (e.g., bad habits, worldly media, treatment of others, etc.) that draw you away from the Spirit? Why is it important to remember that we withdraw ourselves from the Spirit of the Lord, not that He withdraws from us?

MOSIAH 3

V.5: Christ worked many mighty miracles, several of which are listed in this verse. Considering your own life right now, what change or event, regarding yourself or those you know, would you consider a miracle? In other words, fill in the blank of this sentence: "It would be a miracle if _____." Now, concerning that thing, do you have faith that the Lord can bring that to pass if it's God's will? Why or why not?

V.15: Just as the law of Moses "availeth nothing except it were through the atonement of [Christ's] blood," so too does commandment-keeping avail us nothing if it weren't for the Atonement. How can you incorporate the Atonement more into your daily life, especially into your prayer, scripture study, and church attendance?

V.19: What is the hardest part about submitting your will to Heavenly Father, and what helps you to do it?

MOSIAH 4

V.13: How does having the Spirit with you help you live peaceably with others?

V.16: One way this is done (administering our substance to those in need) is through donating fast offerings. How generous are you in your fast offerings? Do you give grudgingly or willingly, and why?

V.19: Thinking of the wealth that you currently have, what people, jobs, and personal skills or characteristics have led to that wealth, and how do you see the hand of the Lord in all those things? Also, thinking of your current spiritual standing, what people, experiences, and spiritual gifts have led to your testimony and commandment-keeping, and how do you see the hand of the Lord in that as well?

MOSIAH 5

V.2: Obeying the gospel of Jesus Christ can change not just our behaviors but also our actual desires. How have you seen your desires change throughout your life so that you "have no more disposition to do evil, but to do good continually"? If you're desiring sin in your life right now, what can you do to bring the Spirit more fully into your life so that those desires become more righteous?

V.7: What similarities do you see between physical birth and spiritual birth, and why is birth an appropriate analogy for being converted? What feelings do parents experience when they have a child, and how might this be similar to how Christ feels when we make covenants with Him?

MOSIAH 6

V.1–2: What do you remember about when you made your baptismal covenant, and what feelings did you have? What about the first time you went through the temple to receive your own endowment and make the related covenants (if you have done so)? What about when you entered into the sealing covenant (if you have done so)?

MOSIAH 7

V.12–13: Ammon showed great respect toward King Limhi and forgave him for the misunderstanding based on Limhi's lack of knowledge. How do you resolve misunderstandings with family members, Church members, and others? Why is it important to have respect and forgiveness toward them?

V.20: The first step of repentance is to recognize that you've done something wrong, which is what King Limhi does in this verse. Why is this so hard to do? What helps you to admit that you're wrong, both to God and to others?

V.30: Chaff is the inedible casings of corns and grasses that are usually tossed away for their worthlessness or given to animals as fodder. Why can the things of the world never satisfy our spiritual appetites? What can the gospel of Jesus Christ give us that no worldly thing can?

MOSIAH 8

V.20–21: What are some reasons that we stray from the true Shepherd, Jesus Christ, and wander into worldly paths that spiritually destroy us? What makes people spiritually blind? How can you personally avoid these things, especially considering your weaknesses and how you tend to sin?

MOSIAH 9

V.1: How does choosing to see the good in others affect our relationships? Thinking about your own family members, what good traits do they have that you admire the most?

V.17: What "enemies" do you have right now, including sins, weaknesses, and trials? Thinking of those things specifically, how do you think the Lord can strengthen you and help you overcome them?

MOSIAH 10

V.9: Every man that could bear arms, both young and old, was expected to fight. What good have you seen brought about by the elderly in the Church? What good is brought about by the younger generation?

V.11: Is there anything in your life right now that you're trying to do with your own strength instead of with the Lord's? If so, why? How can you more fully invite the Lord's strength into your life?

MOSIAH 11

V.3–4: The people of Zeniff were brought into this financial and spiritual bondage not because of outside conflict (the Lamanites) but because of inner turmoil (King Noah). Likewise, today many members of the Church are led away from Christ not just by outside sources but by ideas proposed by apostate members (or active

members who hold apostate beliefs). What are some examples you have seen of this? How can you protect yourself against false doctrine from both members and non-members of the Church?

V.18–19: How would you respond to someone who says the following: "Your church says that I'm living in sin right now. Well, if that's true, then why am I so happy and successful in my life?"

MOSIAH 12

V.18–19: Some people ask questions about the gospel out of a sincere desire to learn and know for themselves, but others (like these priests) ask questions with the intent of attacking, finding fault, and diminishing the confidence of the one who is answering. How do you react when someone questions your faith sincerely, and how do you react when someone does it with animosity? What do you think the Lord wants you do in each of these circumstances?

V.31–32: How would you respond to this similar question: "Doth salvation come by reading scriptures, saying prayers, and going to church?" Why or why not?

MOSIAH 13

V.1: Abinadi, like Jesus Christ, was judged to be mad, or crazy, by those whose sins he testified against. What are some accusations that people in the world today have toward members of the Church who are firm in living their beliefs? What gives you the strength to stand strong despite these attacks?

V.13–14: These verses describe both the justice and mercy of Heavenly Father. What role do each of these play in the plan of salvation, and how does the Atonement of Jesus Christ fit in with these characteristics of God?

MOSIAH 14

V.6: This verse symbolizes that we all need the Savior because we are all imperfect. How would you respond to someone who says they don't need the Savior because they've lived a good enough life?

V.7: Why is a lamb or sheep an appropriate symbol for Jesus Christ?

MOSIAH 15

V.1: Abinadi didn't just read his audience the Isaiah passage and expect them to understand; he summarized it in his own words, explained its messages, and testified of its truth. How can parents, teachers, missionaries, and others implement this teaching tool, and why is it so important?

V.19: There are some who believe that following Jesus Christ is *a* way of life, but Abinadi and others plainly teach that He is *the* way, and the *only* way, to salvation. How would you explain this, and the reasons behind it, to someone of a non-Christian faith?

MOSIAH 16

V.9: What are all the ways in which light is used? With these uses in mind, in what ways is Jesus Christ the Light of the World?

MOSIAH 17

V.4: How do you record what is said in church meetings, both by the speakers and by the Spirit? If you do not record anything, how could doing so bless your life?

V.20: Many people use the story of Abinadi and his one convert, Alma, to prove how missionary work can be a success even with very few baptisms. (Alma ended up converting hundreds of others, and his descendants included many other influential Book of Mormon writers.) However, why would Abinadi's mission have been a success even if Alma *didn't* get baptized?

MOSIAH 18

V.1: One reason Alma was able to preach repentance unto the people is because he himself experienced it. How has repentance blessed your own life, and how would you explain this to a nonmember?

V.9: What is more difficult for you and why—to bear the burdens of and mourn with others, or to let others bear your burdens and mourn with you? Why are both important requirements of members of God's Church?

V.26: How has service in the Church increased the Spirit and knowledge of God in your life?

MOSIAH 19

V.11–12: Though nobody is commanding men to leave their wives and children today, what influences in the world have the potential to take a man or woman away from his or her spouse and children physically, spiritually, mentally, and emotionally? How can you protect yourself from and not give in to these influences?

MOSIAH 20

V.6–11: This entire conflict could have been avoided if the Lamanites and the people of Limhi had just communicated. How does communication prevent and resolve problems, especially in family life? How would you describe what perfect communication is like? How can you improve your own communication skills, especially in a situation like this when somebody offends you?

V.11: The people of Limhi were motivated by thoughts of their lives, their wives, and their children. What motivates you to "exert yourself" every day in the war between good and evil, and why?

MOSIAH 21

V.6–12: The Nephites suffered great loss because they tried several times to deliver themselves out of bondage before turning to the Lord. Why do we so often wait to consult the Lord when we have trials? Why do we in general, and you in particular, try to do things on our own instead of turning to Him?

V.26: The finding of the Jaredite record and the arrival of Ammon and his brethren happened within a relatively short period of time, both of which served as answers to their prayers for deliverance. What are some specific things you've been praying for in your life, and what answers have you seen and felt recently?

MOSIAH 22

V.2: In what ways can we physically and spiritually distance ourselves from sin? Why is it better to avoid sin and temptation than to fight against it when it comes?

MOSIAH 23

V.12–13: The message of Alma to his people was basically the message found in Galatians 5:1: "Stand fast therefore in the liberty wherewith Christ hath made us free, and be not entangled again with the yoke of bondage." When you repent of a sin or overcome a weakness, what helps you to forsake it instead of returning to it?

V.18: How well do you watch over and nourish "with things pertaining to righteousness" those people over whom you have influence, including your children, those you minister to, and those related to your calling? What resources do you use to provide nourishment?

V.27–28: Instead of hushing the people's fears for them, Alma encouraged them to look toward the Lord and find peace in Him. How can you apply this principle to service and parenting?

MOSIAH 24

V.11–12: God knew the circumstances of the people of Alma and accepted the prayers of their hearts. In addition to praying morning and evening and at mealtimes, when, where, and how could you also pray during the day so that you stay close to the Lord?

V.14: This was the reason for the afflictions of the people of Alma: "That ye may stand as witnesses for me hereafter, and that ye may know of a surety that I, the Lord God, do visit my people in their afflictions." Considering the trials that you have gone through, what testimony or witness can you bear to others about the Lord's power and love?

Mosiah 25

V.10: When have you seen the "immediate goodness of God" recently in your life? How is He blessing you right now?

Mosiah 26

V.1–3: What feelings might be felt by parents who have wayward children? How might Satan attempt to discourage them? What truths of God can bring them comfort?

V.5: Like in many cases today, the Nephites here seem to have been influenced by their social circles. How have friends influenced you (or someone you know) throughout life, for good or for bad? Is there anything regarding friends in your life right now that needs to be changed in order to maintain the Spirit in your life? How can you be a better friend and positively influence those around you?

V.15–19: In the Lord's response to Alma, He spends five verses comforting him and praising him and his people for their righteousness before actually answering his stated question. How can you follow this example when others come to you for help or advice? How good are you at comforting others, and how can you improve?

V.30: What does the phrase "as often as my people repent" mean to you? How does this verse apply to overcoming weaknesses?

Mosiah 27

V.6–7: Is there a specific time in your life when you especially felt peace and prosperity? What brought you to that point?

V.9: Is there anything in your life, especially in your media usage, that is "giving a chance for the enemy of God to exercise his power over" you? What do you need to do to minimize the power of Satan in these things and maximize the power of God in your life?

V.22–23: Alma and his priests fasted with very specific purposes in mind. How good are you at fasting with a purpose? What was the goal of your most recent fast, and how did you see the Lord's hand regarding it? What would be a good goal for your next fast?

Mosiah 28

V.2: The Lamanites were wicked because of the iniquity that was passed down to them through the generations. Are there any bad traditions that have been passed down to you (disobeying a certain commandment, holding an opinion contrary to the prophets, etc.)? How can you overcome these things in your life so that they don't continue on to your posterity?

V.2: How does knowledge of the Savior cure us of hatred and help us be friendly to one another?

MOSIAH 29

V.8–9: When Mosiah considered the future of his son Aaron, he took his pat into account. While it's not always wise to dwell on past mistakes, it is wise to learn from them and try to protect ourselves from them in the future.[11] What do you need to be careful about in your life so you don't "backslide" (see Jeremiah 3:22) toward your past sins and mistakes?

V.10: Looking forward to your own future, what do you need to do now (regarding school, work, family, church, or any other important sphere of your life) that will help you have peace in the future?

"Before we can write the gospel in our own book of life, we must learn the gospel as it is written in the books of scripture."

—Elder Bruce R. McConkie[12]

THE BOOK OF ALMA

ALMA 1

V.4: Satan often mixes lies with truth. What truths of the gospel are represented in this verse? Where are the lies? What are some similar philosophies or teachings you've heard about in today's world?

V.25: When have you needed to "stand fast in the faith" and be "steadfast and immovable in keeping the commandments of God," especially when others were not keeping the commandments? What do you think helped these people to "[bear] with patience the persecution which was heaped upon them"?

ALMA 2

V.3: How active are you in participating in the political process of your country? Why is it important to be actively engaged in such civil affairs?

V.21: By understanding Satan's "plans and . . . plots," we too can guard ourselves against him and preserve ourselves and our families from being destroyed. What are some of Satan's tactics to lead people to sin? What tactics are you especially vulnerable to (i.e., what are your weaknesses) that you need to watchful about and avoid?

ALMA 3

V.1–2: The Nephites suffered tremendously because of the poor choices of others. What are some of the trials people face (or you personally have faced) as a result of others' agency? How can the Atonement help people in this situation?

V.4: What role does our appearance play in identifying us as a follower of Christ or a follower of the world? What have the prophets taught us regarding how we should look and dress?

ALMA 4

V.14: What feelings do you have when you consider "the resurrection of the dead, according to the will and power and deliverance of Jesus Christ from the bands of death"? How often do you consider that sacred and joyous truth? How does it affect the way you live?

V.15: The phrase "the Spirit of the Lord did not fail him" reminds us of the Holy Ghost's great power to comfort and guide us in our afflictions. How does the Holy Ghost lift your spirits when you are feeling sorrowful? How does He help you know what to do when faced with a difficult problem?

ALMA 5

V.19: What does it mean to have "a pure heart"? What does it mean to have "clean hands"? How are they connected?

V.22: Where and how are worldly influences likely to make their way into our lives and "stain" them? How are you doing at keeping the filthiness of the world out of your mind, heart, and home?

V.37: What are some ways in which the Lord calls after us? How does He most often try to get *your* attention? Why is it sometimes difficult to hear His voice, and why is it sometimes difficult to obey it?

V.50: What do you do differently in your home to prepare for the arrival of an important person? What can you differently in your life to prepare for the coming of the Lord Jesus Christ?

V.59: How does the Savior drive out our spiritual enemies? What resources has He given us to protect us from evil? How much are you taking advantage of those resources, and what impact is it having on you?

ALMA 6

V.6: Who are some people in your life "who know not God" for whom you could pray and fast? What are you doing to participate in missionary work?

ALMA 7

V.3: What does God's grace mean to you personally? What impact has His grace had on you throughout your life?

V.12: Christ experienced everything personally so that He could understand and comfort every person individually. How does it make you feel to know that Christ perfectly understands your situation, your trials, and your infirmities? Knowing that, how do you think He could give you comfort and direction in your life right now?

V.23–24: On a scale of 1 to 5, how would you rank yourself in each of these attributes—humility, submissiveness, gentleness, patience, long-suffering, temperance, diligence in keeping the commandments, asking God for what you need, thanking God for what you have, faith, hope, and charity? For those on which you ranked low, what could you do to develop these attributes in yourself?

ALMA 8

V.1: What do you do to not get "burned out" from doing good works in your life? What are some examples of wholesome ways to rest? Why is it important that we take time to rest?

V.10: What do you think it means to "wrestle with God in mighty prayer"? What are some aspects of prayer that take great concentration, effort, and strength? What are some things that you sincerely pray for?

V.26: How we treat the servants of God says much about who we are and what we value. What do you do to sustain and support your Church leaders and the local missionaries? What more could you do to support them?

Alma 9

V.10: How does the Lord deliver us out of sin, temptation, trials, sorrow, and other mortal ailments? (Consider each of these things separately.) Is there anything holding you down in your life right now that you could look to the Lord for deliverance from?

V.11: How have you experienced the power, mercy, and long-suffering of God in your own life? How are you doing at being long-suffering toward others and yourself, and what can you do to improve?

Alma 10

V.1–3: It seems from these verses that Amulek found a sense of identity from his family history. What are some of your favorite stories from your own family history? How has your family heritage shaped your identity?

V.11: What commandments and teachings of the gospel have been a blessing to you and your family? How can you teach your children that living the gospel brings great blessings?

V.28–30: The people of Ammonihah were angry with Amulek and planned to remember his words to use against him. In relationships (though this is a different context than this verse), how can remembering past mistakes or offenses of a person harm a relationship? What helps you to "forgive and forget" when a friend or family member offends you?

Alma 11

V.24: What are some examples in our day of putting money above God? What other things might we put above God in our lives, and why? What does it mean to you to put God first in your life?

V.30–31: How would you answer Zeezrom's question about how you know what you know about the gospel? How would you explain to someone else how they could learn that the gospel is true?

Alma 12

V.1: How well do you think you know the scriptures? Are you able to "explain" and "unfold" the scriptures in teaching settings? What's one area that you lack in, for example a specific standard work or doctrine, that you could seek to improve?

V.7: How do you think the "thoughts and intents of [your] heart" are right now? What righteous thoughts and desires guide you on a daily basis? Are there any unrighteous thoughts or motivations that have crept into your mind and heart that you ought to change?

V.25: How would you simply explain the plan of redemption to a child or a nonmember? What is your personal testimony about its truthfulness and impact on your life?

ALMA 13

V.5: How is the priesthood connected with the Atonement of Jesus Christ? How has the priesthood helped you personally to develop a relationship with Jesus Christ and experience the blessings of His atoning sacrifice?

V.15: Why has God required His children to pay tithing, even since the very beginning? What blessings have you seen in your own life from paying a full and honest tithe? If you're struggling to pay tithing right now, what makes it difficult for you, and what could you do to work toward paying a full tithe?

V.21: What are some reasons people may procrastinate repentance? Why is it better to repent now rather than put if off until later?

ALMA 14

V.10–11: How is our temporal perspective of death different than the spiritual perspective we gain by knowing the gospel of Jesus Christ? Though it is difficult for those they leave behind, what do the righteous experience when they leave this life? How can the Lord help those who mourn their loss?

V.28: Alma and Amulek had great power granted unto them "according to their faith which was in Christ." What are some situations in life in which we need to have the power of God to succeed? Why does faith in Jesus Christ offer such great power?

ALMA 15

V.13–14: In your experience, what motivates people to be baptized? What motivates people to stay strong and active in the gospel and Church of Jesus Christ? Why did you get baptized, and what has motivated you to keep the faith?

ALMA 16

V.13–14: How do we sometimes fall into the trap of preaching the gospel "with respect of persons"? What thoughts and teachings can help us to preach to everyone, as Alma and Amulek did, "without any respect of persons"?

V.16: What do you think are some ways that the Spirit prepares the minds and hearts of people to accept the gospel? How does knowing the role of the Holy Ghost in conversion change the way you approach missionary work?

ALMA 17

V.9: What are some ways the Lord has used you, or is currently using you, to accomplish His purposes? How does the Spirit help us be effective instruments? Why did the sons of Mosiah believe they could successfully convert the Lamanites, even though most Nephites at that time thought that they were beyond redemption?

V.25: Why is service such an effective missionary tool? When have you seen service soften the hearts of nonmembers to hear the message of the gospel? What service opportunities are there around you in which you could participate?

Alma 18

V.11: What are some different reasons people might not want to communicate with God? What keeps you from communicating sincerely with Him? What kind of relationship does He want us to have with Him, and why?

V.28–30: Why is it important to answer questions simply, clearly, and briefly when sharing the gospel? How would you simply and briefly describe the following things: the Book of Mormon, the Restoration of the gospel, prophets, the Atonement, and the steps of the gospel of Jesus Christ?

Alma 19

V.1–5: King Lamoni's wife knew very little and yet believed anyway. What helps you to have faith even when you don't know all the answers? How does Satan try to diminish our faith when there are things we still don't know?

V.23: What does it mean to you to trust your child "unto the Lord"? How can parents exercise faith in the Lord while raising their children?

V.29–30: Two women, Abish and King Lamoni's wife, played vital roles in this miraculous story of the conversion of the Lamanites. What important roles do women play in homes and in the Church? What women in your life are especially inspiring to you, and why?

Alma 20

V.8–12: How can a person's conversion to the gospel sometimes lead to strained relationships with family and friends? What advice would you give to a recent convert who is experiencing this?

V.24: Ammon here, like in many instances, thought about others more than about himself. How selfless do you consider yourself to be, and how can you be better? What are some ways in your life right now that you can put others' well-being above your own?

Alma 21

V.6: How would you explain the need for repentance to someone who doesn't think they need to repent? What testimony could you share with them about your experiences with repentance? What invitations could you extend to them?

V.11: When discussing the gospel with others, what is the "right" way to teach to avoid the spirit of contention? What are some things that invite the spirit of contention, and why are these ineffective teaching methods?

Alma 22

V.14: What feelings do you have as you ponder the truth that "the sting of death should be swallowed up in the hopes of glory"? If you have had friends or loved ones pass away, how does it make you feel knowing that they will live again?

V.33–34: The Nephites did their best to keep the Lamanites in one place and guard their lands against them. What are some things we can do to minimize the influence of Satan in our lives? What are some of the major ways he tries to attack us, and how can we guard ourselves against those attacks?

ALMA 23

V.16–17: Just as the converted Lamanites took upon themselves a new name, we also take upon ourselves the name of Christ when we are baptized. What does it mean to you to take upon yourself the name of Christ? How does it distinguish you from those who have not taken upon themselves the name of Christ through baptism?

ALMA 24

V.7–9: This king and his people reacted with humility and even gratitude to being told of their sins and the sins of their fathers. How do you usually react when you realize that you've sinned? What happens when we react with defensiveness or despondence? What happens when we react with humility and gratitude? Why is being convinced of your sins actually something you could thank God for?

V.11: This verse contains the phrases "all that we could do" and "all we could do," and v.15 uses the phrase "as much as we could do." In what ways is repentance really "all you can do"? Also, what do you think it means "to get God to take [our sins] away from our hearts," and what can we do to make this happen?

ALMA 25

V.6: The people who previously mocked and cast out Aaron and his brethren were now "stirred up in remembrance" of their words. How can this story bring hope and comfort to full-time and member missionaries? What can happen in the life of an individual to make them interested in the gospel of Jesus Christ, even when they had previously rejected it?

V.16: How does your faith in Jesus Christ help you to have hope in the future? How does studying the scriptures help strengthen that faith and hope?

ALMA 26

V.23–24: President Thomas S. Monson recalled the following story: "During the 1940s and 1950s, an American prison warden, Clinton Duffy, was well known for his efforts to rehabilitate the men in his prison. Said one critic, 'You should know that leopards don't change their spots!' Replied Warden Duffy, 'You should know I don't work with leopards. I work with men, and men change every day.'"[13] Do you believe that anyone can repent and change? Why or why not? How are our lives different, both in our relationships with others and our relationships with ourselves, when we believe that anyone can change?

V.37: God cares about all people, no matter their gender, race, nationality, social circumstances, economic status, mental ability, educational opportunities, career choice, or any other categorization we often use to judge others. How well do you unconditionally love others? Is there anything in the list above or otherwise that influences the way you look at and treat others?

If so, what thoughts are behind that prejudice, and what thoughts can help you overcome that prejudice?

ALMA 27

V.7: What are some decisions that are good to "inquire of the Lord" about? How has He helped you make important decisions in your life so far? What decisions are you facing right now that you could inquire of the Lord about?

V.8: This verse is about restitution and making amends for sins we have committed, especially against other people. What do you think restitution accomplishes, both for the sinner and for the one who was sinned against? What are some examples of sins that we may commit in our daily lives, and for each of these sins what would restitution look like?

ALMA 28

V.8: Like the journey of these missionaries, our life journeys are often full of sufferings, sorrows, and afflictions *as well as* joy and safety. What can we do so that the joy outweighs the sorrow? How can we maintain a positive attitude even during difficult trials? Why do you think mortality includes such a wide range of experiences that evoke such a wide range of emotions?

ALMA 29

V.10: How can sharing the gospel help us remember how the Lord has blessed us? How do you feel when you see those you love "coming to the Lord their God," and what are some specific examples of this in your life?

V.13: What calling, if any, do you hold right now? How has the Lord given you success in it? What about it brings you joy?

ALMA 30

V.4–5: Would you consider your life to be more peaceful or stressful right now? If peaceful, what can you thank the Lord for? If stressful, what can you ask the Lord to help you with?

V.24: Korihor claims that faithful members of the Church are in bondage, whereas those who don't subscribe to its teachings are free. Why is the opposite of this actually true? In other words, how does living the gospel increase one's freedom, and how does not living the gospel lead people into bondage?

V.42: What are some ways, big or small, that we "put off the Spirit of God that it may have no place in [us]"? How does following the Holy Ghost reduce the power that Satan has over us? What's one thing you could change in your life in order to feel the Spirit more strongly, or in other words, to "make place" for Him?

ALMA 31

V.4: Why is it a "great loss" when somebody becomes less active in the Church? If you were reaching out to a less-active member, how could you let them know that they are wanted and needed at church?

V.9: How well do you think *you* are doing at "observing to keep the commandments of God"? What is a commandment that you're particularly good at, and how have you come to be so obedient to it? What is a commandment that you struggle with, and what can you do to improve?

V.22: Instead of pridefully thanking God that we're "chosen," what could we humbly thank Him for?

ALMA 32

V.26–27: What "experiments" might you do in your life in order to learn about the truthfulness of certain gospel principles? How has "experimenting on the word" helped you develop your testimony?

V.38: What can cause us to neglect living the gospel of Jesus Christ, especially when it comes to daily scripture study and prayers? What are some examples of "when the heat of the sun cometh and scorcheth" us in our lives? Why is it better to turn toward God during times like this instead of away from Him?

ALMA 33

V.5: For many people in ancient times, their field was their livelihood and how they provided for their families. With this in mind, how has the Lord helped you in your jobs and career, either in finding work or in having success at work? What could you ask Him for that would help you with your work right now?

V.20: What are some reasons why people in our day doubt and reject Jesus Christ? Where might people "look" instead of the Savior to try to find help and healing? Why will these sources ultimately be insufficient and ineffective?

ALMA 34

V.14: Why is it important that "the whole meaning" of our commandment-keeping points "to that great and last sacrifice . . . [of] the Son of God"? How can we do this with our prayers, scripture study, and church attendance? How are those aspects of our lives different when we focus them on the Atonement of Jesus Christ versus when we don't?

V.26: Where can you go to engage in private, quiet introspection as you converse with God in prayer? What does it mean to "pour out your soul" to Him? How can you do better at talking *with* Him instead of just talking *to* Him?

V.40–41: When experiencing afflictions, what's the difference between bearing them with patience versus without patience? What things personally test your patience? What are a few steps you can take to develop the Christlike attribute of patience?

ALMA 35

V.13: The Nephites were willing to go to war rather than cast out the Zoramite converts. Sometimes we too face great trials because of our righteous choices. What are some examples of this, perhaps from your own life? How does the Lord support those who choose the right, even when the world doesn't support them?

ALMA 36

V.16: Alma describes the guilt he suffered for the sins he committed. How would you describe the feelings of guilt that you have when you sin?

How can these feelings lead us toward God if we choose? How can they lead us away from God if we choose?

V.20: Alma describes the joy he felt upon receiving forgiveness. How would you describe the feelings you have when you repent and feel God's forgiveness? When was the last time you felt this, and what was that experience like?

V.26: What can teachers (including missionaries and parents) do so that those they teach can "taste," "see," and "know" for themselves? Why is this better than simply relying on the testimony and experiences of the teacher?

ALMA 37

V.7: One application of this scripture is found in looking at young missionaries and the "salvation of many souls" that they bring about. Why does the work of the Lord still progress when done by what the world would call immature and unlearned young missionaries? Why is this a better system than sending highly educated and mature missionaries out to preach the gospel?

V.37: What are some of the "doings" in your life right now that you can counsel with the Lord about, and how do you suppose He can "direct thee for good"? How do consistent and sincere morning and evening prayers lead us to eventually "be lifted up at the last day"?

ALMA 38

V.8: Do you recall an experience when you cried unto the Lord and "did find peace to [your] soul"? What was that experience like?

V.12: How often do you engage in idleness? What are some things that cause you to waste away your time, and what leads you to do so? Thinking of these things, what steps could you take to be more diligent and "refrain from idleness"?

ALMA 39

V.12–13: Alma told Corianton to both "refrain from your iniquities" and "turn to the Lord with all your mind, might, and strength." When we are trying to forsake a sin, why it is vital to replace it with the things of God? What are some good things you can fill your life with as you strive to avoid and overcome sin?

V.18: Why is it necessary for us to know about the plan of redemption? How do our lives change when we truly understand and have a testimony of this plan?

ALMA 40

V.1: How do you think Alma was able to perceive that Corianton was worried about the Resurrection? What can parents do to notice, discern, and understand the needs and worries of their children, and why is this important?

V.5: Alma didn't know all the answers about the Resurrection, but he knew the most important things. What are some other examples in the gospel where there are still unanswered questions? Considering these things, why is okay that we don't know the answers yet, and what are the core doctrines that we *do* know that we ought to hold fast to?

Alma 41

V.5–6: Why do you think God judges us not just by our works but by our desires also? What are some righteous desires you have, and why do you desire those things? What are some less-than-righteous desires you have, and what can you do to curb these desires and make your desires more righteous?

Alma 42

V.7: Why is it necessary for our progression that we are able to "follow after [our] own will"? How have your choices helped you become the person you are today?

V.11: Consider, as Alma does here, what things would be like "if it were not for the plan of redemption." How would our view of death be different? How would our view of life be different?

Alma 43

V.2: How can "the spirit of prophecy and revelation" help you in your missionary work? What experiences have you had when you've received revelation about who to share the gospel with, what to share, or how to share it?

V.11–13: Because the Anti-Nephi-Lehies had promised not to fight, the Nephites helped them keep their resolution by defending them. What can you do to help others follow through on their resolutions and achieve their goals? Are you aware of any specific goals that your friends or family have right now? If so, how can you support them in these things?

Alma 44

V.9: When people look at you, your talents, and your achievements, what might they attribute your success to? What could you do to glorify God in all your endeavors, instead of glorifying yourself?

V.20: Though Moroni felt anger (see v.17), he also exhibited great self-control by ceasing the fight as soon as the Lamanites surrendered. How can self-control protect us from Satan and his influence? How well are you at controlling your emotions, especially in tense situations, and how can you be better?

Alma 45

V.10: The word *dwindle* in "dwindle in unbelief" signifies a gradual apostasy. Why is it more common for people to gradually fall into unbelief rather than to quickly lose their testimony? How might this happen to someone in our day? What can you do to strengthen your faith if you notice your testimony dwindling?

V.15: Alma gave priesthood blessings to his sons. How have priesthood blessings helped you throughout your life? When was the last time you received a blessing, and what impact did it have on you? Is there anything troubling you right now that may be made lighter with the help of a priesthood blessing?

Alma 46

V.20: What blessings have you noticed in your life from making and keeping covenants with God?

V.23: The Nephites found inspiration in the stories of their ancestors, specifically Joseph. What stories do you know from your family history that inspire you?

V.39–41: These verses note a sense of spiritual confidence when leaving this life. The people "firmly [believed] that their souls were redeemed by the Lord Jesus Christ," and "we must needs suppose" that "those who died in the faith of Christ are happy in him." Do you have that same confidence about your own salvation—that if you die while striving to be faithful, then you will receive joy and eternal life? Why or why not? How do you think God wants us to feel about our future salvation?

ALMA 47

V.1: Like Amalickiah, there are many who dissent from the Church and then seek to spiritually attack those who remain in the Church. What examples of this have you seen, and why do you think people do this? Is there anyone you've had to distance yourself from, or that you *should* distance yourself from, because of their antagonism toward the Church and desire to lead people away from it?

V.6: These Lamanites were "fixed in their minds with a determined resolution" not to fight the Nephites. In the next chapters, however, they end up doing just that. Why do you think it's not enough to just mentally decide ("fixed in their *minds*") to do or not do something? What else is needed to truly withstand temptation and accomplish our goals?

ALMA 48

V.7: Instead of just preparing his armies to fight, Moroni had been "preparing the minds of the people to be faithful unto the Lord their God." In other words, he put spiritual things before temporal things. How can we prioritize spiritual things in our own lives? What often stops us from doing this? How is your life different when you're focused on spiritual things versus temporal things?

V.12: Moroni's heart "did swell with thanksgiving to his God" for the privileges and blessings that the people enjoyed. What are some things that make your heart swell with thanksgiving to God, and why?

ALMA 49

V.1–2: The city of Ammonihah had been rebuilt and fortified. What are some ways we might need to "rebuild" our lives after repenting? Why is it important that we actually *change* something in our lives as part of the repentance process, instead of just asking God for forgiveness?

V.8: Moroni instructed the Nephites on how to prepare for battle. How can parents and Church leaders help youth to be spiritually prepared for the life ahead of them? What other preparation might be important, and how can parents and leaders help youth in these areas as well?

V.13: Moroni had fortified "every city in all the land round about." Consider the cities as a metaphor for different attributes of your character: faith, hope, charity, virtue, knowledge, patience, humility, diligence, and obedience. In which of these attributes are you strongest, and which need to be strengthened and fortified?[14] What are some specific things you can do to strengthen the characteristics that are currently weak? Why is it important to be as strong as possible in *all* of these areas?

ALMA 50

V.12: Moroni's armies "did increase daily because of the assurance of protection" they offered. Likewise, the membership of the Church grows as people notice the spiritual protection it offers. What specifically might a nonmember notice about members and the Church in general that would draw them toward learning more and becoming a member? If you were asked by somebody, "What could your church offer me?" how would you respond, especially by drawing on your personal experiences?

V.35: "Stubborn" is a great way to describe Morianton and his people. What are some ways that people, including yourself, can be stubborn? Why do you think people can be so stubborn? What are the negative consequences of stubbornness, and what can we do to diminish this trait in ourselves?

ALMA 51

V.1–3: Like the king-men in this chapter, there are many people today, both inside and outside the Church, who "desire that a few particular points of the" Church and the gospel be altered. What examples of this have you seen? Why do they want to change these parts of the gospel? Why do Church leaders not alter these things, and what would happen if they did?

V.29–32: Nephite reinforcements finally arrived, giving them an advantage over the Lamanites. What reinforcements can you turn to (people, things, and actions) when you're having a hard time in your life with trials or temptations? How have these reinforcements helped you in the past?

ALMA 52

V.5: Because of "the enormity" of the number of Lamanites, Teancum thought it was not expedient to attack them in their cities. What can happen if we try to do too many things at once, like overcome *all* our weaknesses, reach *all* our goals, or start *all* the good habits we'd like to start? What do you think is a better strategy for accomplishing these things, and why?

V.18–19: With the arrival of Moroni, the highest military leaders held a "council of war" to discuss war strategies. What are some things a family may need to discuss during a family council to improve their circumstances, and why is it important to do this in a council setting instead of just individually? Are there any questions or issues in your own family life right now that could be resolved with the help of a family council? If so, how could you bring it up?

ALMA 53

V.5: Moroni knew that if he kept the Lamanites busy with labor, they wouldn't have the time, energy, or opportunity to retaliate or strategize about how to break free. What can happen in our lives, especially spiritually, if we are overly busy? How does Satan try to keep us so busy that we don't have time for the most important things? What could you cut back on in your life in order to focus on what matters most, like your spiritual development and spending quality time with family?

V.12–13: What are some things that people have done for you, or sacrificed for you, so that you would be spiritually and physically safe, even if they had "afflictions and tribulations" because of it? How could you show your gratitude for these people?

ALMA 54

V.17: Many conflicts can be tied back to misunderstandings, which can lead to resentment. What should you do when misunderstandings arise in your own life, for example with family members or Church leaders? What can you do to rid yourself of feelings of resentment and contention when they arise?

V.19: Just as Ammoron claimed not to fear Moroni, there are people today who claim not to fear God, for example by claiming He doesn't exist or believing He is lenient. Why *should* we fear God? What is the difference between fearing God and being afraid of God, and why should we strive for the former while avoiding the latter?

ALMA 55

V.8–12: The Lamanite guards used the phrase "we are weary" twice as the reason they wanted to drink the wine so badly. How does weariness, physically or spiritually, affect our ability to make good choices? What can you do to avoid becoming physically weary? What can you do to avoid becoming spiritually weary?

V.31–32: The simple phrase "If their wine would poison a Lamanite it would also poison a Nephite" teaches us that immoral behaviors are dangerous to everyone. What are some things, especially in the media, that people usually feel are inappropriate for children? Why are these things harmful and inappropriate for all ages?

ALMA 56

V.16–17: When in your life have you felt "depressed in body as well as in spirit" but had your spirits lifted by someone else? What could you do to help a friend who's feeling depressed?

V.47–48: How have you been positively influenced by your mother (or another female role model in your life)? What can parents do so that their children can say, "We do not doubt that our [parents] knew it"?

ALMA 57

V.1–4: Helaman refused to compromise with Ammoron and claimed an easy victory because of it. How does Satan try to get us to compromise our values and standards? What happens when we begin to make moral compromises? What happens when we stay true to our values and standards?

V.36: Helaman just suffered a tremendous loss, with a thousand of his men slain. Yet here he is, "filled with exceeding joy because of the goodness of God in preserving" them. How can you develop this kind of attitude of gratitude, even (or especially) when going through difficult trials? What effect can gratitude have on people during their trials?

ALMA 58

V.11: Even when the Lord doesn't immediately deliver us from our trials, He can give us "assurances" and "speak peace to our souls" in the midst of them. When was the last time you felt the Spirit bringing you peace, and what were the circumstances? What peace and assurances do you stand in need of right now?

V.40: Consider these traits of the stripling warriors: they remembered the Lord daily, obeyed the commandments continually, and had faith in the words of the prophets. How are you doing in each of these areas? What could you do to improve in each of these areas?

ALMA 59

V.9–10: The phrase "it was easier to keep the city . . . than to retake it" can be better understood with the saying, "It's better to prepare and prevent than to repair and repent."[15] Why is it better—and ultimately easier—to avoid sin than to engage in it and then repent? What would you say to someone who claims, "It's okay for me to sin—I'll just repent later"?

ALMA 60

V.6–7: Why are we often neglectful about helping those who are suffering in the world, physically or spiritually? What things do people spend their time doing that bring them into a state of "thoughtless stupor"? What are the biggest time-wasters in your own life, and how could you spend that time more productively?

V.20: What are some times in your life when the Lord has delivered you (for example, from sin or trials)? How does it help you to remember these times?

V.21: What "means" has the Lord given you—talents, material blessings, spiritual gifts, etc.—to help others? What's one way you can use these means right now to accomplish God's work?

ALMA 61

V.15: Pahoran sought God's help ("according to the Spirit of God") with a temporal matter (conducting the war). How can the Spirit help us in our temporal endeavors? When have you experienced this? What temporal matters are you involved with now in which God could help you if you asked?

V.19: Pahoran managed to experience joy despite being censured. When other people treat us poorly, what can we do to still feel joyful and feel love toward those people?

ALMA 62

V.2: How do you feel when you hear of people not living the gospel, especially Church members who rebel against God and apostatize? How do you handle these feelings?

V.37: It was said of Teancum that he "had fought valiantly for his country" and that he was "a true friend of liberty." What do you think people will say about you when you die? What would you like them to say?

V.41: Trials will often either harden us or soften us. Who do you know who has been hardened by their trials, thus moving away from God?

Who do you know who has been softened by their trials, thus moving closer to God? How do you usually react to trials, and what can help you to stay humble and faithful to God during hard times?

Alma 63

V.1–2: These verses first describe Shiblon as someone who kept the commandments and strove to do good. Then it says "and also did his brother," meaning Corianton, the one who had previously been involved in immorality (see Alma 39:3). How do these verses help us to see the "big picture" of Corianton's life? Who do you know who is similar to Corianton—who made mistakes but returned to righteousness? How should we treat people who have seriously sinned in the past?

"Don't yield to Satan's lie that you don't have time to study the scriptures. Choose to take time to study them. Feasting on the word of God each day is more important than sleep, school, work, television shows, video games or social media. You may need to reorganize your priorities to provide time for the study of the word of God. If so, do it!"

—Elder Richard G. Scott[16]

THE BOOK OF HELAMAN

HELAMAN 1

V.14: What weapons does Satan use in today's world? Which of them do you fear the most, and why? How can you protect yourself and your family from his attacks?

V.31–32: The Lamanites had trusted Coriantumr to lead them, but instead he "plunged the Lamanites into the midst of the Nephites." How can bad friends plunge us into dangerous situations? What advice would you give to the youth of the Church about choosing friends wisely?

HELAMAN 2

V.1: Like in the time of Helaman, our day is also filled with contention concerning politics. How have you seen political contention? Why is this a negative thing, and how can we avoid it—especially when we have strong opinions about certain issues?

HELAMAN 3

V.15: What are some different ways you could keep a record of your life? Which do you think would work best for you, and why?

V.28: Who might we be tempted to shut the "gate of heaven" on? Why does God keep it open?

V.35: What is something you can do every day to "wax stronger and stronger in [your] humility, and firmer and firmer in the faith of Christ"? Plan out exactly what, when, where, and how you plan to do this.

V.37: In what ways have you been blessed by the examples of your parents or others who have influenced you?

HELAMAN 4

V.21–23: These verses describe what can be seen as a chain of events: the people were stiffnecked, ignored the commandments, sought to change the commandments, and disbelieved in revelation. How is this pattern found among Church members today? What can you do to avoid this?

V.25: What does it mean to you to cleave unto God?

HELAMAN 5

V.12: What "shafts" and "hail" have you been protected from in your life because of your foundation built upon Jesus Christ?

V.26: The message to "fear not" is found often in the scriptures. Why does God want us to "fear not"? How does your faith help reduce your fear?

V.41: This verse teaches us to "repent . . . *until* you have faith," meaning that you don't have to wait until you have faith before you repent. How does repentance increase our faith in Jesus Christ? How does our repentance and faith make darkness disappear from our lives?

HELAMAN 6

V.3: How have you experienced fellowshipping in the Church, both on the receiving end and on the giving end? Who do you think would benefit from greater fellowshipping from you?

V.4: If you were to recount to someone your conversion experience, what would you say?

V.35: How can you tell when the Spirit starts to withdraw from you? When you notice it happening, what can you do to get Him back?

HELAMAN 7

V.17: Consider the powerful question here: "Why will ye die?" Now consider a few sins, both in general and things you may struggle with. Why do people tend to do these things? What do they gain from it? On the other hand, what are the consequences of doing these things, and how do they lead to spiritual death?

V.27: Wo means sorrow. Why does sin bring misery, and why does righteousness bring joy?

HELAMAN 8

V.17: How does Jesus's life bring you gladness and joy? If you had the chance to witness any part of His mortal ministry, what would it be and why?

V.25: What are some "treasures in heaven" that we should be striving for and investing in during our lives? What could you do to better focus on these things?

HELAMAN 9

V.10: How can the death of a loved one sometimes encourage people to seek God? What could you say to someone to comfort them after such a loss?

V.20: What are some ways people lose their integrity because of the love of money? When faced with a choice to be dishonest and gain something from it, what helps you to choose honesty instead?

HELAMAN 10

V.1: Despite feeling that Nephi was a prophet, the people dispersed without acting on those feelings. What are some reasons we don't always act on what we feel? How can you combat these obstacles to make sure you're being a "doer" of the word and not just a "hearer" (see James 1:22)?

V.16: How can the Spirit protect us in dangerous situations, both physically and spiritually? When have you have felt the Lord's protection?

Helaman 11

V.16: God loves us so much that He is willing to "try again" and again to see if we will serve Him, always granting forgiveness after sincere repentance. How does that make you feel and change the way that you live?

V.23: What doctrines help people live peaceably one with another?

V.25: Like these robbers, Satan is stealthy and hides well.[17] How have you noticed this?

Helaman 12

V.4: What "vain things of the world" are you most likely to set your heart upon, and why? What can you do to avoid or resist this temptation?

V.17: The term "move mountains" is often used to demonstrate God's power. What are some figurative mountains (trials) in your own life that would be a miracle to move? How do you think God, with His infinite power, could help you?

Helaman 13

V.3: What are some times when we need to rely on God to know what to say? When have you experienced the Spirit putting thoughts into your heart?

V.25: One thing that people often do with any sin is to try to justify it. What are some justifications for common sins in our day? Why is justification spiritually dangerous?

V.29: Think about your day-to-day life. What opportunities do you have to choose light versus darkness? How does it feel when your life is full of light versus full of darkness?

Helaman 14

V.8: How does faith in Christ lead us to everlasting life? What does it mean to you to believe on the Son of God?

V.30: We are free to choose how we live our lives, no matter what direction Satan or God are pulling us. As one phrase goes, "God votes for you, the devil votes against you, and you cast the deciding vote." With this in mind, what do you truly want for yourself in this life and the next? How will you use your agency to achieve that?

Helaman 15

V.10: What are some experiences you've had in which you've felt "enlightened" and changed the way you lived because of it?

V.14–16: God judges us based on what we know, and He holds us more accountable when we know more. Therefore, we can't ever truly judge someone because we don't know how much they know and how well they're living in accordance with it. When might you be tempted to judge someone's actions and spirituality? What should you be doing instead?

Helaman 16

V.2: What metaphorical stones and arrows are shot at us when we share the gospel? How can the Spirit of God protect you from these?

V.14: Great revelation can and does come to the spiritually mature. What could you do to increase your *worthiness* to receive revelation and increase the *likelihood* of receiving revelation?

"The Savior asked questions that invited learners to think and feel deeply about the truths He taught. Our questions can similarly inspire learners to ponder gospel truths and find ways to apply them in their lives. An inspired question is an invitation to learners to discover gospel truths on their own and to evaluate their understanding of and commitment to those truths."

—Teaching in the Savior's Way[18]

THE BOOK OF THIRD NEPHI

3 NEPHI 1

V.12: When was the last time you "cried mightily unto the Lord"? What were the circumstances, and how did He respond?

V.30: Why might some parents "decrease in faith and righteousness" when their children make poor choices? What advice would you have for a parent in this position? How would you encourage them to increase in faith and righteousness instead?

3 NEPHI 2

V.2: How do some people nowadays look at the doctrine of Christ as "a foolish and vain thing"? What is your personal testimony about the doctrine of Christ?

V.3: Disbelief often goes hand in hand with iniquity. Why is this? How does disbelief foster sin, and how does sin foster disbelief?

V.17: What do you do to drive out sins and bad habits when you notice them? What helps you to notice them in the first place?

3 NEPHI 3

V.12–14: Lachoneus combined sincere prayer with diligent action. How could you apply this principle right now?

3 NEPHI 4

V.10: When have you felt that you've done something in the strength of the Lord? How does this feel compared to when it's just your own strength?

V.19–20: Relying on the things of the world, without God's help, will eventually leave us destitute. Why can we never be truly satisfied by worldly pleasures? Why does worldly pleasure eventually always run out?

3 NEPHI 5

V.1: What spiritual experiences have you had that have strengthened your testimony and left little room for doubt?

V.26: What does it mean to you to know your Redeemer? How is it different than knowing *about* Him? How has your relationship with Him developed throughout your life?

3 Nephi 6

V.15: How does pride act as a "gateway sin" for other iniquities? How does seeking power and authority hinder our spiritual progression?

V.18: What do you think is the will of God concerning you today, this week, this month, this year, and this lifetime? How well are you living in accordance with this, and how can you be better?

3 Nephi 7

V.12: Satan often tempts people with promises of prosperity in exchange for iniquity. In what ways might he do this today? How can you stop such thoughts if they come to you?

V.16: Nephi was overcome with his desire to preach. On a scale of 1 to 10, how would you rate your desire to share the gospel? What could you do to increase that desire, and why should you?

V.17: What wonderful experiences have you had while ministering? This could mean when you have served or taught others, or when others have served or taught you.

3 Nephi 8

V.1: What miracles can Church members bring to pass in our day? What miracles have you seen?

V.1: How does someone become cleansed "every whit" from his or her iniquity?

3 Nephi 9

V.9: What are some things that destroy our peace? What can we do to keep these out of our hearts and homes?

V.18: What does it mean to you that the Lord is "Alpha and Omega"? How has He acted as a light to you?

3 Nephi 10

V.4: This verse refers to God's actions of nourishing the people in the past. How has God nourished you in the past?

V.7: The origin of the word *desolate* comes from the words "thoroughly alone" or "abandoned." How does gospel disobedience lead to us being thoroughly alone?

3 Nephi 11

V.37–38: How does being like a little child lead us toward eternal life? Who are some people in your life who embody the traits of a little child?

V.39: What are some ways we can build our lives upon the doctrine of Jesus Christ? How has doing so protected you from "the gates of hell"?

3 Nephi 12

V.5: What does it mean to you to be meek? How does the world think you need to be in order to be successful, and how does this differ from being meek?

V.7: How can you incorporate mercy into your day-to-day life?

V.25: This verse encourages us to make things right with people as soon as possible, including apologizing and making amends when necessary. The next time you are in a contentious situation with someone, what can you do to quickly resolve it?

3 NEPHI 13

V.1: What are some ways we might "do [our] alms before men," either on purpose or even accidentally? Why are we tempted to do so?

V.7: Consider the things you say most often in your prayers. How can you make these things more meaningful?

V.25: What does it mean to you to minister? What does it mean to the people you are assigned to minister? How can you better minister to those you are assigned to so that it is more effective for them?

V.27–30: How prone are you to worry? Why do you worry? How do these verses help you to be calmer and worry less?

3 NEPHI 14

V.3–4: What are some "motes" you tend to notice and judge in others? What "beams" in yourself should you focus on instead?

V.19: What "good fruit" have you brought forth in your life so far? What goals do you have for your future about what you could do for the Lord and for the world?

3 NEPHI 15

V.9: What does it mean to you to endure to the end? What helps you to do this?

V.19–20: How does iniquity prevent us from receiving and understanding the word of the Lord?

3 NEPHI 16

V.5: The gathering of Israel includes perfecting the Saints, redeeming the dead, and preaching the gospel. What's one goal you could set in each of these areas to more fully participate in this great work?

3 NEPHI 17

V.4: Just like the lost tribes weren't lost to the Father, those who feel lonely and isolated from others aren't isolated from God. How can a strong relationship with God help you when your relationships with others are struggling?

V.21–22: How can you follow the Savior's example of focusing on people "one by one"? How can you follow His example of loving children and seeking to bless them?

3 NEPHI 18

V.14: How have you been blessed by keeping the commandments the Lord has given you, both generally (to the whole Church) and personally (through personal revelation)?

V.16: What's one aspect of the Savior's example that stands out to you that you would like to emulate? What can you change in your life to better follow Christ's example in this thing?

V.32: This verse, and this whole chapter, makes it clear that *everyone* is welcome at our church meetings. What are some types of people you might feel uncomfortable with at church? What could you do to minister to these types of people?

3 NEPHI 19

V.6: How can prayer help us prepare for church and other spiritual activities? What are some things you can ask for in such prayers, for example before your scripture study?

V.9: What would your life be like without the gift of the Holy Ghost? With that in mind, what are you most grateful for about the gift of the Holy Ghost?

3 NEPHI 20

V.35: "All the ends of the earth shall see the salvation of the Father" through missionary work. How would you define your sphere of influence when it comes to missionary work? Who do you interact with and in what settings? How can you implement missionary work more into your daily life?

V.38: What is the "naught" that we sell ourselves for? In other words, what are the motivations behind your sins? How can knowing this help you to avoid sin in the future?

V.42: What are some things you are involved with right now that are important to you? Now imagine the Lord being with you in these things—how does that make you feel?

3 NEPHI 21

V.9: What are some reasons people don't believe the message of the Restoration when they hear it? How would you respond to each of these concerns?

V.19: What dishonesty, envy, contention, or immorality exists in your life that needs to be done away with? How will you do this?

3 NEPHI 22

V.7–8: What helps you to remember God's kindness and mercy even when you may feel unworthy of it? How does knowing about God's "everlasting kindness" make a difference in the repentance process?

V.17: What Church doctrines are most under attack right now? What weapons have symbolically been formed to attack these things? How has the Church responded in defense of the truth?

3 NEPHI 23

V.11–12: What gets in your way of consistently keeping a journal or recording spiritual experiences? What are some specific things you can do to overcome these barriers?

3 Nephi 24

V.3: The process of purifying and purging is difficult but necessary for our spiritual progress. What's the hardest thing for you about being called to repentance? What's your favorite thing about the spiritual purifying and purging process?

V.10: What blessings have you received—both spiritually and temporally—from paying a full tithe? If you are full tithe payer right now, what blessings could you ask the Lord for, drawing upon your obedience to this commandment? If you're not a full tithe payer, how do you think your life would be blessed by paying a full tithe?

3 Nephi 25

V.3: With the Lord's help, we can tread down wickedness. Pick one unrighteous aspect of your character or actions that you'd like to change. How can you and the Lord work together to tread down this thing?

3 Nephi 26

V.13: The people were tremendously blessed to hear the Lord for three days. At general conference, we are blessed to hear the voice of the Lord for two days. What can you do before, during, and after general conference to make it as spiritually effective and powerful as possible?

V.18: Why do you think it's important to keep some spiritual experiences sacred? How can you know what's appropriate to share with someone?

3 Nephi 27

V.3–4: Consider the names that the Church has been known by during this dispensation, such as the Mormon Church and the LDS Church. Why do you think these names came about and persisted for so long? What difference does it make to call the Church by its divinely appointed name—The Church of Jesus Christ of Latter-day Saints?[19]

V.29: While "asking" just requires asking God for help, "knocking" requires doing action our part. What is something that you want God's help with right now? How can you ask Him for help with this thing, and what personal efforts can you put forth to achieve it?

3 Nephi 28

V.11: How has the Holy Ghost testified to you of the Father and the Son?

V.34: Consider the doctrine in this verse that rejecting the Lord's prophets is the same as rejecting the Lord. What doctrines do people sometimes struggle with when it comes to following the prophet? Is there anything you personally struggle with? How can somebody come to know that the prophet is truly the Lord's spokesperson?

V.36–37: Mormon had a question, and God answered it with clear knowledge. When has this happened to you? What question would you like God to answer right now?

57

3 Nephi 29

V.2: Sometimes we may feel as if the Lord is delaying blessings for us. When have you needed to exercise patience as you've waited for blessings? Why do you think it sometimes takes a long time for the Lord's promised blessings to be fulfilled?

V.3: Imagine you're going through a hard time and are starting to doubt, thinking that you're living the gospel in vain. What would you write to your future self in that situation to provide encouragement and knowledge?

3 Nephi 30

V.2: Consider the seriousness of the sins in this verse. If the Lord is willing to forgive these kinds of sins if people repent, what does that say about your own sins if you repent? Think about replacing the sins in this verse with a list of the sins and weaknesses that often plague you. How do you feel when you consider the Lord's willingness to forgive you for even the grossest sins?

THE BOOK OF FOURTH NEPHI

4 NEPHI 1

V.2: This verse shows the pacifying effect of the gospel on relationships. How has living the gospel positively influenced your relationships? Or how do you notice your relationships struggle when you struggle with the gospel?

V.12: How are you blessed by attending church (i.e., "meeting together oft")? Why is it important to go to church every week rather than just every once in a while?

V.16: If you were to write a list of past sins or weaknesses that you have overcome, what would be on that list? What feelings do you have as you consider how far you've come spiritually with the Lord?

V.46: The spiritual downfall of this people is evidence that "the love of money is the root of all evil" (1 Tim. 6:10). Why do you think this is? How can the love of money lead people away from the gospel of Jesus Christ in our day?

"My dear brothers and sisters, I promise that as you prayerfully study the Book of Mormon every day, you will make better decisions—every day. I promise that as you ponder what you study, the windows of heaven will open, and you will receive answers to your own questions and direction for your own life. I promise that as you daily immerse yourself in the Book of Mormon, you can be immunized against the evils of the day."

—President Russell M. Nelson[20]

THE BOOK OF MORMON

MORMON 1

V.2: This verse shows that even children can be quite spiritually mature. What people have you known who have impressed you at a young age? How can adults help children develop their spirituality and reach their spiritual potential?

V.15: Like in verse 2, the word *sober* is used to describe Mormon. What do you think this word entails, and what is its opposite? Why is soberness a good quality to have?

MORMON 2

V.14: When you are feeling angry at God because of your circumstances or the consequences of your sins, what thoughts can help you develop a broken heart and a contrite spirit instead?

V.19: In this verse, Mormon expressed his confidence of being "lifted up at the last day" and saved. How confident are you regarding your own salvation, and why?

MORMON 3

V.1: What is one spiritual thing and one temporal thing you can do today to better prepare for the future?

V.9–10: Great tragedies can cause people to hold grudges and seek revenge. How can doing this be spiritually destructive? What advice would you give someone in such a predicament?

MORMON 4

V.15: Even though this is a natural and understandable response to such a tragedy, what do you think God would have wanted them to feel and do? What do you think God wants you to learn from your trials right now, or from the tragedies you've experienced?

MORMON 5

V.6–7: The Nephites were no match for the Lamanites with just their own strength. What are some circumstances that are difficult to face on our own but are made manageable with the help of the Lord?

V.10: Do you know "from whence [your] blessings come"? Think of some of the talents you have and the things you've achieved. If somebody asked you how you have been able to do [insert accomplishment], how could you respond in a way that properly gives the glory to God?

Mormon 6

V.17: Mormon maintained a clear vision of the worth of these people despite their sins, calling them "fair ones." How can you do the same when looking at others who are sinning? How can you keep this attitude about yourself when sinning?

V.17: Imagine Christ standing a little way off from you with His arms wide open. How can such an image help you to repent when needed? What image might Satan try to portray instead?

Mormon 7

V.1: Mormon just witnessed the Lamanites utterly destroy his people, yet he still had charity for them and wanted the best for them in the future. What conflicts or offenses can cause people's love for others to diminish? When someone offends us, what can help us maintain a desire for their well-being, and why is this important to do?

Mormon 8

V.15: What does it mean to you to do something "with an eye single to [God's] glory"? Considering the things you're involved with right now, what does this mean in your situation?

V.24: What have you accomplished in your life by your faith in Jesus Christ? What current endeavors in your life will require your faith for you to be successful in them?

V.31: One of Satan's greatest tactics is to minimize the seriousness of sin, saying "Do this, or do that, and it mattereth not." When such thoughts are presented to you, how can you respond to them?

Mormon 9

V.20: What does it mean to you to trust in God? What are some things you need to trust Him about right now?

V.22: When was the last time you shared the gospel, and what was that experience like? What can you plan to do next to share the gospel?

V.28: What are some specific temptations you face that you could ask for help with, especially in your morning prayers? How do you think doing this will help you?

"The scriptures are described as 'quick and powerful.' The word quick in these verses means 'living.' In other words, the scriptures are alive. Though they were written long ago, they have application today. That makes them powerful. We can profit and learn from them. Likening scriptures to our personal lives will invite inspired thoughts to help us with our modern-day personal experiences." [21]

THE BOOK OF ETHER

ETHER 1

V.35: God answered the brother of Jared's faithful prayer with compassion. When have you felt God's compassion, especially in answering your prayers?

V.36–37: Who are your closest friends, and what specific things could you pray for on their behalf?

ETHER 2

V.1–3: Because of their preparation, the people were able to embark on this journey without fear. What blessings come from being self-reliant and temporally (financially) prepared? When have you needed to rely on your savings, or when might you need to?

V.18: The brother of Jared returned and reported back to the Lord. In your prayers at the end of the day, what could be gained from you doing the same thing, reporting to the Lord about your actions during the day?

V.19: The brother of Jared came to the Lord with two specific problems—light and air. What specific problems do you have right now that you could bring to the Lord in prayer?

ETHER 3

V.3: What are your greatest desires right now? Have you called upon God about these things? Why or why not?

V.5: Imagine being in the future and looking back at your current trials and how the Lord got you through them. With this in mind, do you truly believe that God is able to help you? If there is anything standing in the way of you receiving that help, what can you do to remove that obstacle?

V.15–16: What difference does it make to know that we're created in the image of God?

ETHER 4

V.6: Our ability to receive revelation depends on our worthiness. What's one thing you could change to become more worthy of revelation from the Lord? What revelation do you want most right now?

V.10: What would you say to somebody who doubts that modern-day prophets and apostles are the Lord's servants? What reasons might they have for not believing, and how could you address these concerns?

Ether 5

V.4: How does the Book of Mormon "show forth the power of God and also his word"? How has it brought the power of God into your life to a greater degree?

Ether 6

V.2–3: What are some small and simple things that bring light to your life and make your mortal journey just a little easier?

V.8: It seems that the Spirit never ceases to push us forward. What are some ways you feel that the Lord wants you to move forward right now? This could mean pursuing something new, improving an attribute, developing a new skill, or moving toward a goal. What's one specific thing you can do to move forward with this thing?

Ether 7

V.13: What does forgiveness look like in your own family? In other words, how do you "make up" with each other? What can parents do to teach their children the importance of repentance and forgiveness when it comes to family relationships?

V.23: God sent prophets to warn the people of the specific sins that were plaguing them. If God were to send a personal prophet to your doorstep right now, what do you think he would tell you to do? What can you do to start following that counsel?

Ether 8

V.17: What "fair promises" are promoted by the media to encourage sin, such as immorality and drug and alcohol use?

V.18–19: What reasons can you think of why murder is such an abominable and wicked sin? On the other hand, why do you think the media is so obsessed with it, adding violence and gore to so many movies and TV shows?

V.26: What is one thing you can do to diminish the power of Satan in your life?

Ether 9

V.11: Why are power and money such powerful motivators? Are you tempted by either of these? If so, what is appealing to you about it, and how can you guard yourself from pursuing these above God?

V.26: The book of Ether does a very good job of showing the constant ups and downs of righteousness and wickedness. These are portrayed in extreme ways here, but for us these ups and downs are also very real. What have you noticed about your own spiritual fluctuations? What causes your highs, what causes your lows, and what can you do to stay high for as long and often as possible?

Ether 10

V.1: Shez was righteous, and he had the task "to build up again a broken people." When you realize that your life is "broken" because of the choices you're making, what steps can you take to build it up again?

V.22: How industrious would you consider yourself to be, and how can you be more so? What has helped you learn this principle?

ETHER 11

V.3: How have you been blessed by heeding the words of the prophets? What specific examples can you think of?

ETHER 12

V.4: What are some things you hope for in your personal and family life, in the world, and in the eternities? How can this hope act as an "anchor to your soul" and make you "sure and steadfast, always abounding in good works"?

V.24: In this verse, Moroni does what many of us do—compares himself to others. When do you tend to compare your weaknesses to others' strengths? When you feel tempted to do so, what are some better things you can do instead?

ETHER 13

V.4: Zion is often used interchangeably with the term New Jerusalem. What can you do to make your home and ward more Zion-like?

V.15–17: When faced with dire circumstances, some turn to God while others do not. What do you think goes through the minds of the first group? What about the second group?

ETHER 14

V.1–2: The people were so dependent on worldly things that God cursed the land. What are some material, transitory things we might cleave to because we're so afraid of losing them? What more permanent and lasting things does God want us to cleave to instead?

ETHER 15

V.19: The book of Ether shows that people become corrupted, base, and bloodthirsty creatures when they persist in sin, lose the Spirit, and refuse to repent. What are *you* like when you persist in sin and lose the Spirit? How is this different than when you have the Spirit with you?

V.34: All Ether cared about was being saved in the kingdom of God. He was willing to endure a lifetime of sorrow, and even then, he was humble enough to accept God's will for the remainder of his life. What can you learn from Ether's example, and how can you apply it to your own life?

"There is a power in the [Book of Mormon] which will begin to flow into your lives the moment you begin a serious study of the book. You will find greater power to resist temptation. You will find the power to avoid deception. You will find the power to stay on the strait and narrow path. The scriptures are called 'the words of life,' and nowhere is that more true than it is of the Book of Mormon. When you begin to hunger and thirst after those words, you will find life in greater and greater abundance."

—President Ezra Taft Benson[22]

The Book of Moroni

Moroni 1

V.3: If given the choice to deny Jesus Christ or be killed, what would you choose and why?

Moroni 2

V.2: How has your life been blessed since receiving the gift of the Holy Ghost through God's authorized servants? How strongly do you feel His influence right now, and in what ways?

Moroni 3

V.3: How do you know when you've sufficiently repented and received a remission of your sins?

Moroni 4

V.3: How does the symbol of bread help you better understand the Savior's sacrifice for you? What does bread have to do with the Savior and His Atonement?

Moroni 5

V.2: How does the symbol of wine (or water) help you better understand the Savior's sacrifice for you? What does wine (or water) have to do with the Savior and His Atonement?

Moroni 6

V.4: When have you felt remembered, nourished, and cared for by Church members? How can you do this for other Church members right now?

V.6: Elder Dallin H. Oaks taught, "The ordinance of the sacrament makes the sacrament meeting the most sacred and important meeting in the Church."[23] What can you do to treat this meeting with more reverence and significance?

Moroni 7

V.3: Hope is something that we can have "from this time henceforth until [we] shall rest with [the Lord] in heaven," no matter our circumstances. What helps you to maintain hope, both in good circumstances and in bad?

V.9: What can you do to pray with more "real intent of heart"? What gets in your way of doing this?

V.17: Thoughts of shame and self-hatred are surely from the devil, for they "persuadeth no man to do good, no, not one." When you feel stuck in the trap of thinking negatively about yourself, what can you do to get out of this rut? How can you tell when you get into the rut in the first place?

V.46: What things help you to "cleave unto charity," especially when tempted to act uncharitably? Who is a good example to you of charity, and why?

MORONI 8

V.2: What evidence do you have that God is mindful of you?

V.19–20: Knowing that "the pure mercies of God" ought to be available to children, what can you do to be more merciful, patient, and loving toward the children in your life?

V.29: What spiritual experiences have you had that stand out as being especially influential on your testimony? How do you think God would feel if you were to reject "so great a knowledge" that you've received?

MORONI 9

V.3: How does Satan stir up anger in you, and what are your choices for dealing with it?

V.20: What is the opposite of being "past feeling," and what can you do to obtain such a state of being?

V.25: What are some things in the world that grieve you and weigh you down? How can focusing on the things in this verse—Christ's "mercy and long-suffering, and the hope of his glory and of eternal life"—help lift you up in times of depression?

MORONI 10

V.26: One way to avoid dying in your sins is to repent every day. Looking back at today or yesterday, what do you need to repent of?

V.32: What does it mean to you to be perfected in Christ? How is this different than being perfect?

TOPICAL GUIDE

A

Accomplishment

(See Success)

Accountability

Hel. 14:30; 15:14–16;
Moro. 8:29

Affliction

(See Trial)

Anger

(See also Contention)
Mosiah 12:18–19;
Alma 10:28–30; 44:20;
Morm. 2:14; 3:9–10;
Moro. 9:3

Anti-Nephi-Lehies

Alma 43:11–13

Apostasy of Individuals

Mosiah 8:20–21; 26:1–3;
Alma 45:10; 62:2

Apostasy of the Early Christian Church

2 Ne. 13:1

Apostle

(See Prophets and Apostles)

Atonement

(See Jesus Christ, Atonement through)

Ashamed

Moro. 7:17

B

Baptism

2 Ne. 31:11;
Mosiah 6:1–2; 17:20;
Alma 15:13–14; 23:16–17

Belief

(See Faith)

Bible

2 Ne. 29:3

Bless, Blessing (General)

(See also Bless, Blessing [Personal]; Prosper; Success)
Alma 29:10;
3 Ne. 29:2;
Ether 2:1–3

Bless, Blessing (Personal)

(See also Bless, Blessing [General]; Prosper; Success)
2 Ne. 26:8;
Mosiah 18:1; 25:10;
Alma 10:11; 13:15; 46:20;
Hel. 3:37;
3 Ne. 18:14; 24:10;
4 Ne. 1:12;
Morm. 5:10;
Ether 11:3;
Moro. 2:2

Blind

(See also Hardhearted; Stiffnecked)
Mosiah 8:20–21

Boast

(See Pride)

Boldness

2 Ne. 4:24

Bondage

(See also Deliver)
1 Ne. 14:4;
2 Ne. 1:13;
Mosiah 11:3–4; 21:6–12;
23:12–13;
Alma 30:24

Book of Mormon

1 Ne. 6:4;
2 Ne. 27:14; 29:3; 33:15;
Alma 18:28–30;
Ether 5:4

Burden

(See Trial)

C

Calling

(See also Serve, Service)
1 Ne. 13:37;
2 Ne. 5:26;
Jacob 1:17;
Mosiah 18:26; 23:18;
Alma 29:13

Captivity

(See Bondage)

Career

1 Ne. 18:1;
Jacob 1:17;
Mosiah 4:19; 29:10;
Alma 26:37; 33:5

Carnal Nature

1 Ne. 10:6;
Ether 15:19

Celestial Kingdom

(See Eternal Life)

Change

(See also Change, Invitation to;
Repentance)
1 Ne. 5:21–22; 10:6; 16:36;
Mosiah 3:5; 5:2;
Alma 26:23–24; 39:18; 49:1–2;
63:1–2;
Hel. 15:10

Change, Invitation to

(See also Improve, Invitation to)
Jacob 2:34;
Jarom 1:5;
Mosiah 26:5;
Alma 12:7; 30:42;
3 Ne. 18:16; 21:19; 25:3;
Ether 4:6; 7:23

Charity

(See also Love)
2 Ne. 30:7;
Mosiah 4:16; 28:2;
Alma 7:23–24;
Moro. 7:46

Children

(See also Parents and Children;
Posterity)
Alma 55:31–32;
3 Ne. 11:37–38; 17:21–22;
Morm. 1:2;
Moro. 8:19–20

Choice, Choose

2 Ne. 10:23;
Jacob 7:18;
Mosiah 2:36;

Alma 3:1–2; 35:13; 42:7;
55:8–12;
3 Ne. 1:30;
Ether 10:1

Christlike

1 Ne. 20:10;
Alma 34:40–41

Church Attendance

(See also Ward)
2 Ne. 26:26;
Mosiah 2:3; 3:15; 12:31–32;
17:4;
Alma 34:14; 3 Ne. 18:32; 4
Ne. 1:12; Moro. 6:6

Church Leaders

(See also Leadership; Prophets
and Apostles)
Mosiah 2:11;
Alma 8:26; 49:8; 54:17

Church of God

1 Ne. 14:10; 21:22;
2 Ne. 24:2;
Mosiah 18:9;
Alma 19:29–30; 50:12; 51:1–3;
3 Ne. 22:17; 27:3–4

Church of the Devil

1 Ne. 13:4; 14:10

Comfort

Mosiah 26:1–3; 26:15–19;
Alma 4:15; 7:12; 25:6;
Hel. 9:10

Commandment

(See also Obedience)
1 Ne. 3:5; 13:4;
Jacob 2:34;
Alma 10:11; 31:9; 34:14;
Hel. 4:21–23

Consequence

2 Ne. 28:7–8;
Hel. 7:17;
Morm. 2:14

Contention

(See also Anger)
1 Ne. 18:12;
2 Ne. 21:13;
Mosiah 7:12–13;
Alma 21:11; 54:17;
Hel. 2:1;
3 Ne. 12:25; 21:19

Conversion

Mosiah 5:7;
Alma 20:8–12;
Hel. 6:4

Covenant

Mosiah 5:7; 6:1–2;
Alma 46:20

D

Darkness

1 Ne. 22:13–14;
2 Ne. 30:16–17;
Hel. 5:41; 13:29

Death, Physical

Alma 14:10–11; 22:14; 42:11;
Hel. 9:10

Death, Spiritual

2 Ne. 10:23;
Hel. 7:17

Decision

Alma 27:7; 47:6;
Hel. 14:30

Defend

3 Ne. 22:17

Deliver

(See also Bondage)
Mosiah 21:6–12;
Alma 4:14; 9:10; 60:20

Desire

1 Ne. 16:36;
Mosiah 5:2;
Alma 12:7; 41:5–6; 42:7;
3 Ne. 7:16;
Ether 3:3

Devil

(See Satan)

Difficulty

(See Trial)

Diligence

1 Ne. 10:19;
Jacob 3:11; 5:75;
Mosiah 20:11;
Alma 7:23–24; 8:1; 8:10;
38:12;
3 Ne. 3:12–14; 27:29;
Ether 10:22

Direction

1 Ne. 17:7; 18:1;
Alma 4:15; 7:12; 37:37;
Hel. 14:30

Disobedience

(See also Obedience)
2 Ne. 1:20;
Jacob 2:34;
Mosiah 2:36; 28:2;
Alma 30:24;
Hel. 4:21–23;
3 Ne. 10:7

Doctrine of the Gospel

(See also False Doctrine)
2 Ne. 13:1;
Alma 18:28–30; 40:5; 51:1–3;

3 Ne. 2:2; 11:39; 22:17

Doubt

Alma 33:20;
3 Ne. 2:3; 21:9; 29:3;
Ether 4:10

E

Education

1 Ne. 18:1;
2 Ne. 9:42;
Jacob 1:17;
Mosiah 29:10;
Alma 26:37

Endure

(See also Steadfast)
3 Ne. 15:9

Eternal Life

(See also Salvation)
1 Ne. 7:1–3;
2 Ne. 10:23;
Alma 46:39–41;
3 Ne. 11:37–38;
Moro. 9:25

Example

1 Ne. 8:10;
2 Ne. 5:19; 33:15;
Alma 19:29–30; 56:47–48;
Hel. 3:37;
3 Ne. 11:37–38; 18:16;
Ether 15:34;
Moro. 7:46

Explain

*(Questions focused mainly
on explaining gospel topics or
responding to concerns about the
gospel)*
1 Ne. 15:9;
2 Ne. 3:13; 29:3; 31:11;

Mosiah 11:18–19; 14:6; 15:19;
18:1;
Alma 11:30–31; 12:25; 18:28–
30; 21:6

F

Faith

1 Ne. 3:31;
2 Ne. 18:9–10;
Mosiah 3:5;
Alma 7:23–24; 14:28; 19:1–5;
19:23; 25:16;
Hel. 3:35; 5:26; 5:41; 14:8; 3
Ne. 1:30;
Morm. 8:24

Faithful

(See Steadfast)

False Doctrine

2 Ne. 28:7–8;
Mosiah 11:3–4;
Alma 1:4

Family

*(See also Loved Ones; Marriage;
Parents and Children)*
1 Ne. 5:2–3; 7:1–3; 13:37;
18:1; 18:12; 20:20;
2 Ne. 25:9;
Jacob 6:4;
Mosiah 1:1; 9:1; 19:11–12;
20:6–11;
Alma 10:11; 19:29–30; 52:18–
19; 53:5; 54:17;
Hel. 1:14;
Ether 7:13; 12:4

Family History

Jacob 6:4;
Alma 10:1–3; 46:23

Fast

> Mosiah 4:16; 27:22–23;
> Alma 6:6

Favorite

> 1 Ne. 6:4; 11:28;
> 2 Ne. 19:6; 33:15;
> Alma 10:1–3;
> 3 Ne. 24:3

Fear

> 2 Ne. 8:7–8; 17:1–2; 18:11–13;
> Mosiah 23:27–28;
> Alma 54:19;
> Hel. 1:14; 5:26;
> Ether 14:1–2

Fellowshipping

> *(See also Missionary Work)*
> 2 Ne. 6:11;
> Jacob 7:24;
> Alma 31:4;
> Hel. 6:3;
> 3 Ne. 18:32

Fight

> Mosiah 22:2;
> 3 Ne. 22:17

Firm

> *(See Steadfast)*

Forgiveness

> 2 Ne. 16:7;
> Enos 1:5–6;
> Mosiah 7:12–13;
> Alma 10:28–30; 36:20;
> Hel. 11:16;
> 3 Ne. 12:7; 30:2;
> Ether 7:13;
> Moro. 3:3

Forsake

> *(See also Repentance)*
> 1 Ne. 16:36;

> 2 Ne. 10:23;
> Mosiah 23:12–13;
> Alma 39:12–13; 49:1–2;
> 3 Ne. 2:17; 21:19

Friend

> *(See also Loved Ones)*
> Mosiah 26:5;
> Alma 56:16–17;
> Hel. 1:31–32;
> Ether 1:36–37

Future

> 2 Ne. 17:1–2;
> Mosiah 29:10;
> Alma 25:16; 46:39–41;
> 3 Ne. 14:19; 29:3;
> Morm. 3:1;
> Ether 3:5

G

Gathering of Israel

> *(See Israel)*

Genealogy

> *(See Family History)*

General Conference

> *(See also Prophets and Apostles)*
> 3 Ne. 26:13

Goal

> 1 Ne. 18:1;
> Mosiah 27:22–23;
> Alma 43:11–13; 47:6; 52:5;
> 3 Ne. 14:19; 16:5;
> Ether 6:8

God

> *(See also God, Character of; God, Helping Hand of; God, Justice of; God, Mercy of; God, Mysteries of; God, Power of; God, Relationship with; God, Will of; God, Wisdom of; God, Work of; Jesus Christ)*
> 2 Ne. 7:1; 10:14;
> Mosiah 3:19; 21:6–12;
> Alma 11:24; 19:23

God, Character of

> 2 Ne. 28:7–8;
> Mosiah 13:13–14; 25:10

God, Helping Hand of

> *(See also Comfort; Deliver; Direction; Protection; Strength)*
> 1 Ne. 4:1; 16:23;
> 2 Ne. 4:31; 5:26; 18:9–10;
> Jacob 5:20;
> Mosiah 1:14; 4:19; 9:17; 24:14; 25:10;
> Alma 5:59; 7:12; 9:10; 14:10–11; 27:7; 33:5; 35:13; 37:37;
> Hel. 12:17;
> 3 Ne. 10:4; 20:42; 25:3; 27:29;
> 4 Ne. 1:16;
> Morm. 5:6–7;
> Ether 3:5;
> Moro. 8:2

God, Justice of

> Mosiah 13:13–14

God, Love of

> 1 Ne. 11:8–9;
> Mosiah 24:14;
> Alma 26:37;
> Hel. 11:16;
> 3 Ne. 22:7–8;
> Ether 1:35

God, Mercy of

Jacob 4:7;
Mosiah 13:13–14;
Alma 7:3; 9:11;
3 Ne. 22:7–8; 30:2;
Ether 1:35;
Moro. 9:25

God, Mysteries of

1 Ne. 10:19

God, Power of

1 Ne. 4:1; 17:39;
2 Ne. 7:2–3; 15:5;
W of M 1:14;
Mosiah 3:5; 10:11; 24:14;
Alma 9:11; 14:28;
Hel. 12:17;
3 Ne. 4:10;
Ether 5:4

God, Relationship with

2 Ne. 10:15; 19:6;
Jacob 4:7;
Mosiah 24:11–12;
Alma 13:5; 18:11; 32:38;
34:26; 54:19; 62:41;
Hel. 4:25;
3 Ne. 5:26; 17:4;
Ether 3:15–16; 13:15–17

God, Will of

1 Ne. 8:34; 16:2;
2 Ne. 17:8–9;
Mosiah 3:19;
3 Ne. 6:18

God, Wisdom of

1 Ne. 17:39

God, Work of

2 Ne. 7:2–3; 15:12;
Alma 37:7

Grace

(See God, Mercy of)

Gratitude

Alma 7:23–24; 24:7–9;
30:4–5; 31:22; 48:12; 53:12–
13; 57:36;
3 Ne. 19:9

Great Apostasy

*(See Apostasy of the Early
Christian Church)*

Grief

(See Sorrow)

Guidance

(See Direction)

Guilt

Enos 1:5–6;
Alma 36:16

H

Happy, Happiness

(See Joy)

Hardhearted

(See also Stiffnecked)
Alma 50:35; 62:41

Heal

Mosiah 28:2;
Alma 33:20

Heart

1 Ne. 2:19;
Alma 5:19; 5:22; 12:7; 17:25;
24:11;
Moro. 7:9

Heavenly Father

(See God)

Helping Others

*(See also Fellowshipping; Serve,
Service)*
1 Ne. 1:5;
2 Ne. 13:14–15;
Mosiah 2:11; 18:9; 26:15–19;
Alma 43:11–13; 56:16–17;
60:21;
Moro. 6:4

Holy Ghost

*(See also Holy Ghost, Revelation
through)*
1 Ne. 7:14;
2 Ne. 31:13;
Mosiah 2:3; 2:36; 4:13; 5:2;
18:26;
Alma 4:15; 17:9; 30:42; 61:15;
Hel. 6:35; 10:16; 16:2;
3 Ne. 19:9;
Ether 15:19;
Moro. 2:2

**Holy Ghost, Revelation
through**

1 Ne. 1:16; 2:1–2; 15:9; 17:7;
18:1;
Jacob 4:13;
Enos 1:3;
Alma 5:37; 43:2; 58:11;
Hel. 13:3; 15:10; 16:14;
3 Ne. 5:1; 15:19–20; 18:14;
26:18; 28:11; 28:36–37;
Ether 4:6;
Moro. 8:29

Honesty

Hel. 9:20;
3 Ne. 21:19

Hope

2 Ne. 6:11; 18:9–10;
Alma 7:23–24; 25:6; 25:16;
Ether 12:4;

Moro. 7:3

Humble, Humility

1 Ne. 2:19; 17:39;
2 Ne. 20:7–12;
Mosiah 3:19;
Alma 7:23–24; 24:7–9;
Hel. 3:35;
3 Ne. 12:5;
Morm. 2:14; 5:10

I

Idolatry

2 Ne. 10:14; 12:18;
Mosiah 7:30;
Alma 11:24;
3 Ne. 4:19–20;
Ether 9:11

Immorality

Alma 55:31–32;
3 Ne. 21:19;
Ether 8:17

Improve, Invitation to

1 Ne. 3:22–23;
2 Ne. 16:7; 21:13;
Jacob 6:4;
Mosiah 20:6–11; 26:15–19;
Alma 7:23–24; 9:11; 12:1;
31:9; 34:40–41; 41:5–6; 49:13;
58:40; 60:6–7;
Hel. 3:35

Iniquity

(See Wicked, Wickedness)

Instrument

(See also Serve, Service)
1 Ne. 21:2;
Alma 17:9

Israel

3 Ne. 16:5

J

Jesus Christ

(See also Faith; God; Jesus Christ, Atonement through; Jesus Christ, First Coming of; Jesus Christ, Second Coming of)
1 Ne. 10:6;
2 Ne. 19:6; 22:3; 25:26;
Mosiah 5:7; 14:7; 15:19; 16:9; 28:2;
Alma 7:12; 23:16–17; 33:20;
Hel. 5:12; 14:8;
3 Ne. 9:18;
Moro. 1:3

Jesus Christ, Atonement through

1 Ne. 12:10–11;
2 Ne. 20:26;
Mosiah 3:15; 13:13–14;
Alma 3:1–2; 4:14; 13:5; 34:14;
3 Ne. 8:1;
Morm. 6:17;
Moro. 4:3; 5:2; 10:32

Jesus Christ, First Coming of

1 Ne. 11:28;
2 Ne. 11:7;
Hel. 8:17

Jesus Christ, Second Coming of

Alma 5:50

Job

(See Career)

Joseph Smith

(See also Restoration)
1 Ne. 21:2;

2 Ne. 3:13

Journal Keeping

1 Ne. 9:3–4;
Mosiah 17:4;
Hel. 3:15;
3 Ne. 23:11–12

Joy

1 Ne. 8:10; 22:13–14;
2 Ne. 25:26;
Jacob 5:75;
Enos 1:26;
Alma 28:8; 29:13; 46:39–41;
61:19;
Hel. 7:27; 8:17

Judging Others

2 Ne. 9:42; 26:26;
Alma 26:23–24; 26:37; 63:1–2;
Hel. 3:28; 15:14–16;
3 Ne. 14:3–4; 18:32;
Morm. 6:17

Judgment

Jacob 2:5;
Alma 41:5–6

Justice

(See God, Justice of)

K

Kindness

(See Charity; Love)

Knowledge

Jacob 4:13; 6:12;
Mosiah 28:2;
3 Ne. 28:36–37

L

Language

Jarom 1:5;
Mosiah 20:6–11;
Alma 54:17

Last Days

2 Ne. 28:7–8; 30:16–17

Law

(See also Commandment; Obedience)
Alma 2:3

Law of Moses

Mosiah 3:15

Laziness

2 Ne. 9:27;
Alma 38:12; 60:6–7

Leadership

(See also Church Leaders)
2 Ne. 5:19

Learn

1 Ne. 19:23;
2 Ne. 28:29

Learned

Alma 37:7

Light

Mosiah 16:9;
Hel. 13:29;
3 Ne. 9:18;
Ether 6:2–3

Love

(See also Charity; God, Love of)
Mosiah 7:12–13;
Alma 26:37; 61:19;
Morm. 7:1;

Moro. 8:19–20

Loved Ones

(See also Family; Friend)
1 Ne. 17:47;
Alma 10:28–30; 22:14; 29:10;
43:11–13

M

Marriage

(See also Family; Parents and Children)
1 Ne. 7:1–3;
Mosiah 6:1–2

Materialism

(See also Pride)
Hel. 12:4;
Ether 14:1–2

Media

2 Ne. 15:12;
Mosiah 2:36; 27:9;
Alma 55:31–32;
Ether 8:17; 8:18–19

Mercy

(See God, Mercy of)

Millennium

(See Jesus Christ, Second Coming of)

Miracle

Mosiah 3:5;
3 Ne. 8:1

Missionaries, Full-Time

(See also Missionary Work)
Mosiah 15:1;
Alma 8:26; 25:6; 37:7

Missionary Work

(See also Explain; Fellowshipping; God, Work of; Missionaries, Full-Time; Testimony, Bearing of)
2 Ne. 3:20; 25:26;
Mosiah 17:20;
Alma 6:6; 17:25; 21:11; 25:6;
29:10; 43:2; 50:12;
Hel. 16:2;
3 Ne. 7:16; 20:35;
Morm. 9:22

Mock

(See also Persecution)
2 Ne. 8:7–8;
Jacob 6:8;
Alma 25:6

Money

2 Ne. 9:42; 12:18;
Jacob 2:18–19;
Mosiah 4:19;
Alma 11:24;
Hel. 9:20;
4 Ne. 1:46;
Ether 2:1–3; 9:11

Mortality

1 Ne. 15:35–36; 19:6;
2 Ne. 9:27; 24:11;
Mosiah 1:8;
Alma 28:8; 42:11;
3 Ne. 6:18;
Ether 6:2–3

Motivation

2 Ne. 6:3;
Jacob 2:18–19; 3:11;
Mosiah 20:11;
Alma 12:7; 15:13–14;
3 Ne. 20:38;
Morm. 8:15;
Ether 9:11

Murder

Ether 8:18–19

Music

(See Media)

N

Natural Man

(See Carnal Nature)

New Testament

(See Bible)

O

Obedience

(See also Commandment; Disobedience)
1 Ne. 21:22; 22:30;
2 Ne. 1:20; 31:13;
Jacob 5:75;
Mosiah 3:15; 3:19;
Alma 1:25; 7:23–24; 10:11;
30:24; 31:9; 58:40; 59:9–10;
Hel. 10:1;
3 Ne. 18:14

Old Testament

(See Bible)

Opposite

Morm. 1:15;
Moro. 9:20

Optimism

1 Ne. 16:23; 17:20; 22:13–14;
Mosiah 9:1;
Alma 28:8;
Moro. 9:25

Ordinance

(See Covenant)

Overcome

1 Ne. 3:31; 12:18;
2 Ne. 20:26;
Jacob 5:65–66;
Mosiah 23:12–13; 26:30; 28:2;
Alma 26:37; 52:5;
4 Ne. 1:16

P

Parents and Children

(See also Family)
1 Ne. 3:5;
Mosiah 1:8; 19:11–12; 23:18;
23:27–28; 26:1–3; 28:2;
Alma 10:11; 19:23; 40:1; 49:8;
56:47–48;
Hel. 3:37;
3 Ne. 1:30;
Ether 7:13

Path of the Gospel

Mosiah 15:19

Patience

Alma 1:25; 7:23–24; 9:11;
34:40–41;
3 Ne. 29:2;
Moro. 8:19–20

Peace

Mosiah 1:1; 4:13; 23:27–28;
27:6–7; 29:10;
Alma 30:4–5; 58:11;
Hel. 11:23;
3 Ne. 9:9; 13:27–30

Peer Pressure

1 Ne. 21:22

Perfection

(See Progress, Progression)

Persecution

(See also Mock)
2 Ne. 26:8;
Alma 1:25;
Hel. 16:2

Perseverance

(See Endure)

Plan of Salvation

2 Ne. 8:25;
Jacob 6:8;
Mosiah 13:13–14;
Alma 12:25; 14:10–11; 39:18;
42:11

Poor

2 Ne. 13:14–15;
Mosiah 4:16

Posterity

(See also Parents and Children)
1 Ne. 9:3–4;
Mosiah 28:2

Prayer

1 Ne. 1:5; 4:17; 15:9;
2 Ne. 4:24; 32:9;
Jacob 4:13;
Mosiah 3:15; 12:31–32; 21:26;
24:11–12;
Alma 8:10; 18:11; 32:38;
34:26; 37:37;
3 Ne. 1:12; 3:12–14; 13:7; 19:6;
Morm. 9:28;
Ether 2:18; 2:19;
Moro. 7:9

Premortal Existence

1 Ne. 21:5

Prepare

1 Ne. 7:1–3;
Alma 5:50; 49:8;
Morm. 3:1;

Ether 2:1–3

Pride

(See also Hardhearted; Learned; Materialism; Stiffnecked)
1 Ne. 12:18;
2 Ne. 9:42;
Mosiah 10:11; 21:6–12;
3 Ne. 6:15; 13:1;
Ether 9:11

Priesthood

Alma 13:5; 45:15

Progress, Progression

1 Ne. 18:12; 19:6; 20:10; 21:2;
Alma 42:7;
3 Ne. 6:15; 24:3;
Morm. 1:2;
Ether 6:8;
Moro. 10:32

Prompting

(See Holy Ghost, Revelation through)

Prophets and Apostles

(See also General Conference)
2 Ne. 26:8;
Alma 58:40;
3 Ne. 28:34;
Ether 4:10; 11:3

Prosper

(See also Success)
Mosiah 27:6–7

Protection

1 Ne. 2:1–2;
Mosiah 11:3–4; 19:11–12;
Alma 2:21; 5:59; 22:33–34;
50:12;
Hel. 5:12; 10:16; 16:2;
3 Ne. 11:39

Purity

Alma 5:19

R

React

1 Ne. 16:2;
Mosiah 12:18–19;
Alma 24:7–9; 62:41

Redemption

(See Jesus Christ, Atonement through)

Reject

2 Ne. 27:14;
Alma 33:20;
3 Ne. 28:34

Rejoice

(See Joy)

Relationships with Others

(See also Judging Others)
2 Ne. 10:15; 21:13;
Mosiah 9:1; 20:6–11;
Alma 10:28–30; 26:23–24;
3 Ne. 17:4; 17:21–22;
4 Ne. 1:2;
Morm. 6:17; 7:1;
Ether 7:13

Remember

1 Ne. 17:39;
Alma 10:28–30; 25:6; 29:10;
58:40; 60:20;
3 Ne. 22:7–8

Repentance

(See also Change; Forsake; Guilt)
2 Ne. 14:4; 15:5; 16:7; 31:11;
Mosiah 7:20; 18:1; 26:30;

Alma 13:21; 21:6; 24:11;
26:23–24; 27:8; 36:20; 49:1–2;
59:9–10;
Hel. 5:41;
3 Ne. 2:17; 22:7–8; 24:3;
Morm. 6:17;
Ether 10:1;
Moro. 3:3; 10:26

Resources

1 Ne. 10:19;
2 Ne. 28:29;
Mosiah 23:18;
Alma 5:59; 51:29–32

Restoration

(See also Joseph Smith)
2 Ne. 3:13;
Alma 18:28–30;
3 Ne. 21:9

Resurrection

Alma 4:14; 22:14; 40:5

Revelation

(See Holy Ghost, Revelation through)

Riches

(See Money)

Righteous, Righteousness

2 Ne. 19:18;
Mosiah 5:2; 23:18;
Alma 12:7; 35:13;
Hel. 7:27;
Ether 9:26

S

Sabbath

Jarom 1:5

Sacrament

Moro. 4:3; 5:2; 6:6

Sacrifice

Mosiah 2:3;
Alma 15:16; 53:12–13;
Moro. 1:3

Salvation

*(See also Eternal Life; Plan of
Salvation)*
Mosiah 12:31–32; 14:6; 15:19;
Alma 46:39–41;
Morm. 2:19

Satan

(See also Satan, Tools of)
1 Ne. 16:2;
Jacob 7:18;
Mosiah 27:9;
Alma 30:42;
Hel. 11:25;
Ether 8:26

Satan, Tools of

*(See also Apostasy of Individuals;
False Doctrine; Temptation)*
1 Ne. 14:4;
2 Ne. 1:13; 2:18; 15:12; 28:7–8;
Jacob 7:18;
Mosiah 8:20–21; 19:11–12;
26:1–3; 27:9;
Alma 1:4; 2:21; 5:22; 19:1–5;
22:33–34; 51:1–3; 53:5;
57:1–4;
Hel. 1:14; 13:25;
3 Ne. 7:12;
Morm. 6:17; 8:31;
Ether 8:17

Scattering of Israel

(See Israel)

Scripture Study

(See also Scriptures)
1 Ne. 3:22–23; 19:23; 22:30;
2 Ne. 27:11; 28:29;
Omni 1:17;
Mosiah 3:15; 12:31–32;
Alma 25:16; 32:38; 34:14;
3 Ne. 19:6;
Ether 5:4

Scriptures

*(See also Bible; Book of
Mormon; Scripture Study; Word
of God)*
1 Ne. 5:21–22;
Omni 1:17;
Alma 12:1

Second Coming

*(See Jesus Christ, Second
Coming of)*

Secret Combinations

2 Ne. 30:16–17

Selflessness

Alma 20:24

Serve, Service

*(See also Calling; Helping
Others; Instrument)*
2 Ne. 2:3; 6:3;
Jacob 2:18–19; 5:20; 5:75;
Mosiah 10:9; 18:26; 23:18;
Alma 17:25;
3 Ne. 7:17; 13:1; 13:25

Sharing the Gospel

(See Missionary Work)

Sin

(See Wicked, Wickedness)

Soft, Soften

Alma 17:25; 62:41

Sorrow

1 Ne. 17:47; 22:13–14;
Mosiah 18:9;
Alma 4:15; 9:10; 14:10–11;
24:7–9; 28:8; 56:16–17;
Hel. 7:27;
3 Ne. 10:7;
Ether 15:34;
Moro. 9:25

Spirit

(See Holy Ghost)

Standards

1 Ne. 21:22;
Alma 57:1–4

Steadfast

*(Questions about staying true
to the gospel and maintaining
firm faith amidst trials, temptations, and persecution. See also
Endure; Withstand)*
2 Ne. 26:8;
Mosiah 13:1;
Alma 1:25; 15:13–14; 30:24;
62:41;
Hel. 3:35;
Ether 12:4

Stiffnecked

(See also Hardhearted)
Hel. 4:21–23

Strength

W of M 1:14;
Mosiah 10:11; 13:1;
3 Ne. 4:10

Stress

1 Ne. 5:2–3;
Alma 30:4–5; 44:20;
3 Ne. 13:27–30

Success

(See also Prosper)
2 Ne. 20:7–12;
Mosiah 11:18–19; 17:20;
Alma 14:28; 29:13; 44:9; 52:5;
Morm. 5:10; 8:24

Symbolism

1 Ne. 12:10–11; 17:7;
2 Ne. 1:13; 8:25; 19:18; 31:13;
Mosiah 5:7; 7:30; 14:7; 16:9;
Alma 5:19;
Moro. 4:3; 5:2

T

Talent

1 Ne. 13:37;
Jacob 1:17; 2:18–19;
Alma 44:9; 60:21;
Morm. 5:10

Teach

(See also Explain; Missionary Work)
2 Ne. 5:19; 6:3;
Mosiah 1:8; 15:1; 23:18;
Alma 21:11; 36:26;
Ether 7:13

Temple

1 Ne. 7:1–3; 17:7;
Mosiah 6:1–2;
3 Ne. 16:5

Temporal

1 Ne. 9:3–4;
Alma 14:10–11; 48:7; 61:15;
3 Ne. 24:10;
Morm. 3:1

Temptation

1 Ne. 8:24;

Mosiah 22:2;
Alma 9:10; 47:6; 51:29–32;
Hel. 12:4;
3 Ne. 7:12;
Morm. 9:28;
Ether 9:11

Testimony

(See also Testimony, Bearing of; Testimony, Development of)
Omni 1:17;
Alma 12:25;
3 Ne. 2:2

Testimony, Bearing of

(See also Teach; Missionary Work)
2 Ne. 29:3;
Mosiah 24:14;
Alma 21:6

Testimony, Development of

2 Ne. 31:13;
Mosiah 4:19;
Alma 11:30–31; 32:26–27;
3 Ne. 5:1;
Moro. 8:29

Tithing

Alma 13:15;
3 Ne. 24:10

Trial

1 Ne. 3:31; 4:1; 16:23; 20:10; 21:2;
2 Ne. 4:31; 7:2–3; 18:9–10;
Jacob 3:1;
Mosiah 18:9; 21:6–12; 24:14;
Alma 3:1–2; 4:15; 7:12; 9:10; 28:8; 32:38; 34:40–41; 35:13; 51:29–32; 57:36; 62:41;
Hel. 12:17;
Ether 2:19; 3:5

Trust

2 Ne. 7:2–3; 18:11–13;
Alma 19:23;
Morm. 9:20

Truth

(See Doctrine of the Gospel)

Truth, Difficulty Accepting

1 Ne. 16:2;
3 Ne. 21:9

Type

(See Symbolism)

U

Understand

Mosiah 15:1;
Alma 7:12;
3 Ne. 15:19–20

W

Ward

(See also Church Attendance)
2 Ne. 26:26;
Ether 13:4

Weakness

1 Ne. 16:2; 19:6;
2 Ne. 3:13; 4:31; 7:2–3; 18:9–10;
Jacob 4:7; 5:65–66;
Mosiah 2:11; 9:17; 23:12–13; 26:30;
Alma 2:21; 49:13; 52:5;
3 Ne. 30:2;
4 Ne. 1:16;
Ether 12:24

Wealth

(See Money)

Wicked, Wickedness

1 Ne. 15:35–36; 17:47; 20:20;
2 Ne. 1:13; 7:1; 10:15; 15:5;
15:12; 19:18; 20:26; 23:15;
25:9; 28:7–8; 30:16–17;
Mosiah 8:20–21; 11:18–19;
22:2; 28:2;
Hel. 7:17; 7:27;
3 Ne. 2:3; 7:12; 15:19–20;
20:38; 21:19; 25:3; 30:2;
4 Ne. 1:16;
Morm. 8:31;
Ether 8:18–19; 9:26

Wisdom

(See also God, Wisdom of)
Jacob 6:12

Withstand

(See also Steadfast)
1 Ne. 8:24;
Alma 47:6

Women

Alma 19:29–30

Word of God

*(See also Prophets and Apostles;
Scriptures)*
1 Ne. 8:24;
2 Ne. 28:29;
Alma 5:37; 32:26–27;
3 Ne. 15:19–20;
Ether 5:4

Word of Wisdom

Ether 8:17

Work of Salvation

(See God, Work of)

World, Worldly

1 Ne. 8:34; 17:47; 20:20;
22:13–14;

Mosiah 7:30; 8:20–21; 13:1;
19:11–12;
Alma 3:4; 5:22;
Hel. 12:4;
3 Ne. 4:19–20;
Ether 14:1–2

Worthy

Mosiah 2:3;
Hel. 16:14;
Ether 4:6

NOTES

1 Richard G. Scott, "To Acquire Knowledge and the Strength to Use It Wisely" (Brigham Young University devotional, Jan. 23, 2001), 1, speeches.byu.edu.

2 Henry B. Eyring, "The Lord Will Multiply the Harvest" (address to Church Educational System religious educators, Feb. 6, 1998), 5–6, ChurchofJesusChrist.org.

3 Bruce R. McConkie, *Mormon Doctrine,* 2nd ed. (1966), 137–38.

4 Stephen E. Robinson, "Warring against the Saints of God," *Ensign,* Jan. 1988.

5 *Teachings of the Prophet Joseph Smith,* sel. Joseph Fielding Smith (1976), 304.

6 Spencer W. Kimball, "How Rare a Possession—The Scriptures," *Ensign,* Sept. 1976, 4–5.

7 Boyd K. Packer, "Reverence Invites Revelation," *Ensign,* Nov. 1991, 21.

8 Quentin L. Cook, "Roots and Branches," *Ensign* or *Liahona,* May 2014, 44.

9 Larry R. Lawrence, "Choose Happiness" (Brigham Young University devotional, Mar. 8, 2016), speeches.byu.edu.

10 "Matthew 6–7," *Come, Follow Me—For Individuals and Families: New Testament 2023.*

11 See also Richard G. Scott, "Personal Strength through the Atonement of Jesus Christ," *Ensign* or *Liahona,* Nov. 2013, 83.

12 Bruce R. McConkie, "Holy Writ: Published Anew" (regional representative seminar, Apr. 2, 1982), 2.

13 Thomas S. Monson, "See Others as They May Become," *Ensign* or *Liahona,* Nov. 2012, 68.

14 Consider doing the "Attribute Activity" found at the end of Chapter 6 ("How Do I Develop Christlike Attributes") in *Preach My Gospel.*

15 Ezra Taft Benson, *The Teachings of Ezra Taft Benson* (Salt Lake City: Bookcraft, 1988), 285.

16 Elder Richard G. Scott, "Make the Exercise of Faith Your First Priority," *Ensign* or *Liahona,* Nov. 2014, 93.

17 For example, see David A. Bednar, "Watchful unto Prayer Continually," *Ensign* or *Liahona,* Nov. 2019.

18 "Ask Inspired Questions," *Teaching in the Savior's Way* (2015), 31.

19 For information on this topic, see Russell M. Nelson, "The Correct Name of the Church," *Ensign* or *Liahona,* Nov. 2018.

20 Russell M. Nelson, "The Book of Mormon: What Would Your Life Be Like without It?," *Ensign* or *Liahona,* Nov. 2017, 62–63.

21 "Likening the Scriptures to Our Personal Lives," *Ensign,* Mar. 2009, 34.

22 Ezra Taft Benson, *Teachings of Presidents of the Church: Ezra Taft Benson* (2014), 141.

23 Dallin H. Oaks, "Sacrament Meeting and the Sacrament," *Ensign* or *Liahona,* Nov. 2008, 17.